mod cocktails

*Modern Takes on Classic Recipes
from the '40s, '50s and '60s*

natalie jacob

Creator of Arsenic Lace

PAGE STREET
PUBLISHING CO.

PAGE STREET
PUBLISHING CO.

Copyright © 2019 Natalie Jacob

First published in 2019 by
Page Street Publishing Co.
27 Congress Street, Suite 105
Salem, MA 01970
www.pagestreetpublishing.com

Distributed by Macmillan, sales in Canada by The Canadian Manda Group.

23   22   21   20   19   1   2   3   4   5

ISBN-13: 978-1-62414-829-3
ISBN-10: 1-62414-829-8

Library of Congress Control Number: 2019932130

Cover and book design by Kylie Alexander for Page Street Publishing Co.
Photography by Natalie Jacob

Printed and bound in the United States

To my father for always believing in me.
Wish you were here.

contents

introduction

Today, more than ever, the midcentury look is everywhere. Not just in the case of design and fashion, but also in what people are drinking. The term *midcentury modern* broadly describes architecture, furniture and design from the mid 1930s to the '60s, characterized by clean lines, organic and streamlined forms and lack of embellishment. But what about the drink culture of the time? Undoubtedly, cocktail parties with finger foods, lavish dresses and Hollywood glamour come to mind. So many of the classic drinks that are being enjoyed in cocktail bars all over the world today can be attributed to this very point in time. Many of the cocktails created decades before the midcentury, such as the whiskey-soaked Manhattan or the delightfully refreshing daiquiri, were at the height of their popularity and plenty of drinks—the Moscow Mule, for instance—were being invented. All of these drinks created between the 1940s and 1960s I call "mod cocktails" or midcentury modern drinks.

Two genres of cocktails were popular during the midcentury, the first being the simpler and "classic" drinks in the style of pre-Prohibition cocktails documented in such books as *The South American Gentleman's Companion*, by author and traveler Charles H. Baker, or *The Fine Art of Mixing Drinks*, an encyclopedia of the twentieth-century cocktail, by David Embury. These kinds of drinks, like the daiquiri, Manhattan and old-fashioned, were already familiar. The second genre was a new school of drinks referred to as *tiki*. Tiki can be better understood as Americans' perception of generic island culture during that time. That's because American tiki was not an organic transplantation of Polynesian culture by indigenous people but the brainchild of Ernest Raymond Beaumont Gantt, also known as Don the Beachcomber and Donn Beach. In 1934, inspired by his travels in the South Pacific, Gantt opened Don the Beachcomber, a tropical-themed bar and restaurant, in Hollywood, California. Not too long after, in 1937, Victor Bergeron, also known as Trader Vic, changed the name of the bar he owned in Oakland, California— Hinky Dinks—to Trader Vic's and adopted an island theme inspired by Don the Beachcomber and his own travels. Nearly a decade later, the American craze for all things Polynesian exploded when men returned home from World War II with stories and souvenirs from the islands they'd visited. By the mid- to late 1950s, tiki drinks appeared on menus and at cocktail parties all over the country. Outposts of Don the Beachcomber, Trader Vic's and the many imitations popped up in cities far and wide.

While the tiki movement is currently having the biggest resurgence since it fell out of popularity in the 1970s, I think there is a bit more to be considered in modern times. Tiki is supposed to be fun and built on an idea of escapism, but since it is an American interpretation, there is a level of cultural appropriation associated with it. To enjoy tiki drinks, I don't think we need to imbibe them in a faux-Polynesian setting, out of a porcelain shrunken head. I don't think tiki has to be kitschy or tacky and I don't think these cocktails need to be in their own category. For me, tiki and tropical drinks are just as much "classic" cocktails as, well, classic cocktails. In this book, all these drinks have a home together because they have one thing in common: No matter where or who made them, they all come from the same exact place in time, the midcentury.

In *Mod Cocktails*, I've explored and covered some of the most beloved drinks from these decades, such as the Mai Tai, a drink fought over by the two founding fathers of tiki, Don the Beachcomber and Trader Vic, and more esoteric ones, such as the Arsenic & Old Lace, a floral martini variation. I've also included my original recipes inspired by the drinks from this era. My hope is that there is something for everyone in this book.

For myself, the mid-twentieth century is a magical place in time that I feel most connected to. I'm constantly drawing inspiration from it, not only when developing cocktails, but in every aspect of my life. Whether it's at a flea market furiously searching for rainbow-colored glassware or on a walking tour to lovingly gaze at the inspiring architecture in Palm Springs, I am constantly on the hunt to bring the midcentury into my everyday life.

If you picked up this book, it is probably because you are interested in cocktails or maybe you have an affinity for everything midcentury as I do, or perhaps both. In this book, there are super simple recipes for the beginning at-home bartender and more complicated recipes for someone who might have a little more knowledge and experience. My objective is to change the way we look at these drinks, so we can accept them into our homes and bars with an appreciation for the time and place they come from. The classic cocktails Charles H. Baker and David Embury wrote about can coexist with the drinks of Don the Beachcomber and Trader Vic. These drinks, or "mod cocktails," are midcentury masterpieces that can still be sipped and enjoyed today the same that they were in 1951. So, let's drink, shall we?

mod bar
essentials

Professional bartenders rely on a few simple tools to make great drinks. Setting up your home bar is a lot easier than you may think, and I'll walk you through everything you will need to make the drinks in this book and beyond.

Shaker

There are two main cocktail shakers: a cobbler shaker and a Boston shaker. A cobbler shaker is a three-piece shaker with a strainer built into the top. This type of shaker is great for the at-home bartender, but is not always ideal. My personal favorite, and the one that most professional bartenders use behind the bar, is a two-piece metal Boston shaker. These can normally accommodate more liquid so you can build multiple drinks at a time, and since the shaker is metal, you will be getting the coldest drink possible.

Strainer

There are also two main types of cocktail strainers. A julep strainer is used with a mixing glass for stirred drinks. A Hawthorne strainer, on the other hand, will work with both a mixing glass and a cocktail shaker. When choosing a Hawthorne strainer, make sure you get one with a very tight coil. These are the best and will ensure your cocktails are being strained appropriately. Some bartenders like to double strain their drinks, using a tea strainer. I personally do not do this because I was taught that a little pulp and a few ice chips were crucial elements of a cocktail. If you're using your Hawthorne strainer correctly, pressing down on the gate to block the opening of the strainer should suffice.

Mixing Glass

As for a mixing glass, a simple pint-size (475-ml) glass will do. If you want to be fancy, there are many beautiful crystal mixing glass options on the market. The important thing about your mixing glass when building stirred drinks is that it is chilled before use. I keep my mixing glass in the freezer; that way, it is ready whenever I need to stir something up. Keeping a few cocktail glasses in the freezer for stirred drinks is another great idea. Since stirred drinks are served up with no ice, they tend to come to room temperature a bit more quickly than drinks served on ice. Getting them as cold as possible and keeping them as cold as possible is key.

Jigger

A jigger is probably one of the most crucial bar tools. It makes measuring drinks fast, easy, efficient and, most important, allows you to make consistent drinks. They come in a few varieties, the first being a 1- and 2-ounce (30- and 60-ml) measure; the other being a ½- and ¾-ounce (15- and 22-ml) measure. They now make 1- and 2-ounce (30- and 60-ml) jiggers with markings on the inside that indicate ¼-, ½- and ¾-ounce (7-, 15- and 22-ml) measurements.

Bar Spoon

Having a few good bar spoons on hand is important. You will use these to stir your drinks and crack your ice. I love to stir my drinks with a thinner bar spoon that has a teardrop end. For cracking ice, however, you will need a spoon with a wide bowl. Alternatively, you can crack ice with an ice tapper or a muddler.

Glassware

If you've ever tried to stock your home bar, you've probably been overwhelmed by all the different types of cocktail glasses. It doesn't have to be that complicated and ninety percent of drinks go in a rocks, a Collins or a coupe glass.

For rocks glasses, you'll need both a single and double. A single rocks glass is going to be for anything neat or any spirit on the rocks. The ideal size is between 8 and 10 ounces (237 and 296 ml). A double rocks glass, also called a double old-fashioned, should only be about 2 ounces (59 ml) bigger than a single rocks glass. You can use a double rocks glass for cocktails with ice, of either the shaken or stirred variety, making it a very versatile glass used for many different drinks.

A coupe glass is good for cocktails served "up" meaning shaken or stirred and served chilled without ice, like a martini. A 5½ to 6 ounce (163 to 170 ml) is my favorite size for this type of glass.

A Collins glass is very similar to a highball glass, but there is technically a difference. A highball is a tall, skinny glass, perfect for serving a fizz and a Collins glass is ever so slightly taller and an ideal vessel for serving Collins-style drinks. A 12 ounce (355 ml) glass is my preferred size and can also be repurposed for making tiki drinks that call for crushed ice. Having a few tiki mugs on hand never hurts either.

Ice

Getting good ice at home may be your biggest challenge, but it's not impossible. Many drinks are best with block ice. If you can get your hands on block ice by buying it at a local cocktail bar or ice purveyor, I strongly suggest doing so. This will come in a big block that you can cut down, or it may come in square cubes and longer rectangular cubes for Collins drinks. If getting block ice is out of the question and your quest for the best ice runs deep, you can fill a small cooler with water and let it freeze for a few days. The cloudy stuff will settle at the bottom and you can saw it off (be careful) with a serrated bread knife. You can then tap the big block of clear ice with the knife and it will cause the ice to split. You can keep doing this until you achieve your desired size of ice. Another option is buying silicone ice molds, but you will never achieve clear ice by doing so.

If your freezer has an icemaker that filters water and cracks ice, that should be good enough for stirring drinks. Alternatively, you can hand crack ice cubes by holding a single cube in the palm of your hand and whacking it hard with the back of your bar spoon, or you can crack your ice in a canvas bag made for this purpose.

For fine, snowy ice to use in crushed-ice drinks (see Chapter 5, Frozen & Frosty), I recommend the canvas bag route. If you don't have a canvas ice bag, you can put your ice in a large resealable plastic bag, wrap it in a dishtowel and smash it with a rolling pin or a muddler. This works in a pinch. Regardless of what kind of ice you will be using, it is of the utmost importance to make sure your ice is in a container that has a lid, to prevent the ice from absorbing the flavor of foods in your freezer.

✦

shaken &
citrusy

Shaken drinks are just as delightful today as they were in the past because they are vibrant, aerated, light on the tongue and enjoyable to drink. Bustling with citrusy fizz and tiny little ice chips, there's nothing more refreshing. This style of cocktail includes any drink containing a modifier that isn't clear (juice, cream, eggs) and should thus be shaken hard to appropriately combine all the ingredients. The shaken variety of drinks can be served either up (without ice) in a coupe glass or down (over ice) in a rocks glass, depending on what you're in the mood for. Although shaken drinks existed long before the midcentury, so many delicious recipes came from this era, such as the Hawaiian Room (page 34), a luscious pineapple rum concoction from the 1940s originally served at the Lexington Hotel in New York City.

With shaken drinks, always build all your ingredients in your cocktail shaker and add ice last. This prevents unnecessary dilution to your drink. Shake hard and with as much ice as possible, then strain off the ice immediately. Water content is a big part of what makes a good drink, and it's always important to remember that how the drink is served will determine how long you shake for. If a drink is being served down on ice, it will keep diluting in the glass, so you want to shake for less time. If a drink is being served up without ice, you must shake it longer so that it is reaches proper dilution and stays cold while you're drinking it. A good rule is to shake "up" drinks very hard for about ten seconds and to shake "down" drinks hard for about seven seconds.

Tools of the Trade

To make the drinks in this chapter, you will need a cocktail shaker, a Hawthorne strainer, a citrus peeler and a jigger. The glassware needed is a coupe glass, double rocks glass and a highball glass.

the african queen

My favorite cocktail and probably the most important cocktail of all time is the daiquiri, and the African Queen is one of my own versions of it. The daiquiri (rum, lime, simple syrup) is my gold standard cocktail; it is the first drink I order at any cocktail bar, and if you can master making it, you have earned my trust. Once you know the proper template for a daiquiri or any sour (2 ounces [60 ml] of spirit, 1 ounce [30 ml] of citrus, ¾ ounce [22 ml] of sweetener) the possibilities are endless.

This is a slightly sweeter approach to a traditional daiquiri and the addition of calvados, a French apple brandy, makes it perfect for serving in the fall and colder months. The orgeat and cinnamon add a lot of nutty and warm baking spice notes that make this drink taste like boozy apple pie. This drink is named after the 1951 British-American adventure film starring Humphrey Bogart and Katharine Hepburn.

Makes 1 serving

1½ oz (44 ml) white rum
½ oz (15 ml) calvados
1 oz (30 ml) fresh lime juice
⅜ oz (11 ml) Orgeat (page 184)
⅜ oz (11 ml) Cinnamon Syrup (page 181)
Lime wheel, for garnish

In a cocktail shaker, combine the rum, calvados, lime juice, orgeat and cinnamon syrup. Fill with ice, shake and strain into a coupe glass. Garnish with a lime wheel.

el jefe

If there were ever a city that embodied everything I love, it would be Palm Springs, California. It is a midcentury mecca for design, boasting one of the best collections of modernist architecture in the world. Wealthy clients and celebrities from nearby Los Angeles and across the country commissioned homes in the resort city as part of the movement's boom during the mid-twentieth century. Visiting Palm Springs is like taking a step back to my favorite period of time. While I'm there, my go-to for food and drinks is El Jefe, a Mexican restaurant in the Saguaro Hotel. When I developed this drink, I was inspired by a hibiscus margarita on the menu. Reposado tequila and cinnamon give it baking spice notes, while the mezcal adds a little bit of smoke. It's a sweet, tart and rich margarita variation with an alluring ruby red color. There are few things I love more in life than having a sun-soaked day, lying poolside, eating tacos with a margarita in hand. Sometimes, I just need to close my eyes, take a sip and pretend I'm there.

Makes 1 serving

Dried hibiscus flowers, for rim

Sea salt, for rim

Lime wedge, for rim

1½ oz (44 ml) reposado tequila

½ oz (15 ml) mezcal

¾ oz (22 ml) fresh lime juice

½ oz (15 ml) fresh orange juice

½ oz (15 ml) Hibiscus Syrup (page 182)

½ oz (15 ml) Cinnamon Syrup (page 181)

Freshly grated cinnamon, for garnish

To make the hibiscus sea salt, crush the dried hibiscus flowers in a food processor or coffee grinder. On a small plate, combine the crushed hibiscus flowers with an equal amount of coarse sea salt.

Rim your glass with the hibiscus sea salt by pressing a lime wedge around the edge of the glass and then dipping it into the hibiscus salt.

In a cocktail shaker, combine the tequila, mezcal, lime juice, orange juice, hibiscus syrup and cinnamon syrup. Fill with ice, shake and then strain over ice into your hibiscus salt–rimmed glass. Garnish with freshly grated cinnamon.

hearts on fire

When creating this cocktail, I had two drinks in mind: the margarita and the Tequila Sunrise. Both were probably consumed poolside in what I imagine as a scene reminiscent of a photograph by Slim Aarons, an American photographer famous for capturing socialites, jet-setters and celebrities in the midcentury. In my eyes, the margarita is a perfect specimen of a cocktail, but the Tequila Sunrise, on the other hand, while aesthetically beautiful, is too sugary and sweet. I decided to revamp it and give it some smoke by adding mezcal, Cointreau and lime to make it more margarita-esque, and a rich and spicy hibiscus–habanero syrup in replacement of standard grenadine. The result is smoky and refreshingly citrusy, with floral notes and fruitiness from the hibiscus plus a punch of spice from the habanero.

Makes 1 serving

1½ oz (44 ml) mezcal
½ oz (15 ml) Cointreau or triple sec
1 oz (30 ml) fresh orange juice
½ oz (15 ml) fresh lime juice
¾ oz (22 ml) Hibiscus–Habanero Syrup (page 183)
Lime wheel, for garnish
Tajín seasoning, for garnish

In a cocktail shaker, combine the mezcal, Cointreau, orange juice and lime juice. Fill with ice, shake and strain into a highball glass filled with ice. Pour the hibiscus-habanero syrup down one side of the glass so it sinks to the bottom. This will create a beautiful orange-to-red ombré effect in the glass. Garnish with a lime wheel and a dusting of Tajín on top.

bartender's tip: Tajín is a Mexican condiment consisting primarily of chile peppers, lime and salt. The powder is tangy and spicy and is great for enhancing the flavors of food and cocktails, like a margarita or michelada.

the ghost

This drink, inspired by the coconut drinks of days past, is so simple, but the way the flavors play off one another makes it taste complex. My goal was to make a creamy coconut drink that wasn't overly sweet, that could be citrusy, but also aromatic. Reposado tequila brings oak and vanilla notes that pair with the coconut and muddled strawberries. Fresh lime juice balances the flavors and gives this drink some bite, while rose water adds aromatic, dry floral notes. I named this drink for its ghostlike color, after the 1947 film The Ghost and Mrs. Muir.

Makes 1 serving

½ oz (15 ml) fresh lime juice

3 strawberries, for muddling

1 oz (30 ml) coconut cream

2 oz (60 ml) reposado tequila

¼ oz (7 ml) rose water, for float

Freshly grated nutmeg, for garnish

Strawberry slice, for garnish

Cocktail pick, for skewering the strawberry

In a cocktail shaker, combine the lime juice and 3 strawberries and gently muddle. Next, add the coconut cream and tequila, add ice and shake. Strain into a double rocks glass over ice, float the rose water by pouring it on top and garnish with the nutmeg and the strawberry slice on a cocktail pick.

blue hawaii

The Blue Hawaii wasn't named after the Elvis movie, as you might expect. In fact, the drink predates the movie by four years. Bartender Henry Yee created the cocktail in 1957 while he was working at the Hilton Hawaiian Village in Waikiki. A Bols representative came into the bar and asked Yee to make a drink with the company's blue curaçao liqueur. He delivered a strikingly blue-hued, sweet concoction containing the blue curaçao, rum, vodka and pineapple juice and decorated, of course, with a cocktail umbrella.

Makes 1 serving

¾ oz (22 ml) white rum
¾ oz (22 ml) vodka
¼ oz (7 ml) blue curaçao
½ oz (15 ml) Demerara Syrup (page 180)
1 oz (30 ml) fresh pineapple juice
½ oz (15 ml) fresh lemon juice
Fresh pineapple wedge, for garnish
Cocktail umbrella, for garnish

In a cocktail shaker, combine the rum, vodka, blue curaçao, demerara syrup, pineapple juice and lemon juice. Fill with ice, shake and strain into a double rocks glass filled with ice. Garnish with the pineapple wedge and cocktail umbrella.

pink squirrel

The Pink Squirrel is the Grasshopper's (crème de cacao, crème de menthe, cream, mint) underrated little sister. In recent years, the Grasshopper cocktail has received attention from craft cocktail bars and bartenders, but I think the Pink Squirrel is deserving of a comeback. Invented at Bryant's Cocktail Lounge in Milwaukee, Wisconsin, in the 1950s, it enjoyed a few decades of kitschy popularity before falling into obscurity. It's rich, creamy and bright pink, which makes it a very attractive dessert cocktail. Crème de noyaux is a liqueur made by distilling apricot and cherry pit kernels, combined with bitter almonds and other botanicals. In this drink, it adds a complex, nutty, sweet fruit aroma and flavor with a touch of bitterness. Bryant's originally made it with ice cream and as a milkshake, but I replaced that with cream for a less decadent affair.

Makes 1 serving

1 ¼ oz (37 ml) crème de noyaux

1 oz (30 ml) crème de cacao

1 oz (30 ml) heavy cream

3 Luxardo cherries, for garnish

Cocktail pick, for skewering the cherries

In a cocktail shaker, combine the crème de noyaux, crème de cacao and heavy cream. Fill with ice and shake. Strain into a coupe glass and garnish with the Luxardo cherries skewered on a cocktail pick.

bartender's tip: Luxardo cherries are produced in Luxardo, Italy. These cherries are nothing like the candy-apple red orbs you're use to seeing in dive bars or placed on top of ice cream. They are dense and chewy, with a sweet-tart flavor, and are made with sour marasca cherries preserved in the fruit's famed liquer.

jet pilot

This drink made at Steve Crane's Luau restaurant in Beverly Hills, California, circa 1958, is a variation on Don the Beachcomber's Test Pilot recipe. The Test Pilot is a drink with a combination of rums, falernum, Cointreau, bitters and absinthe. I sometimes wonder whether the bartenders at the Luau looked at the Test Pilot recipe and asked themselves whether Donn Beach was feeling okay the day he invented it. They basically took the Test Pilot recipe and added grapefruit, cinnamon and overproof rum, making it a far superior cocktail and one that more closely resembles that of a Don the Beachcomber drink. Historically, this drink was flash blended with crushed ice for five seconds and then poured into an old-fashioned glass. I prefer to shake this drink with ice and serve it over ice, to prolong the life and integrity of the cocktail. It can afford to be diluted and then sit on ice especially because of the overproof rum in this drink.

Makes 1 serving

1 oz (30 ml) Jamaican rum

¾ oz (22 ml) Puerto Rican rum

¾ oz (22 ml) overproof demerara rum

½ oz (15 ml) falernum

½ oz (15 ml) fresh lime juice

½ oz (15 ml) fresh grapefruit juice

½ oz (15 ml) Cinnamon Syrup (page 181)

2 drops absinthe

Dash of Angostura bitters

Leafy mint sprig, for garnish

3 Luxardo cherries, for garnish

Cocktail pick, for skewering the cherries

Freshly grated cinnamon, for garnish

In a cocktail shaker, combine the rums, falernum, lime juice, grapefruit juice, cinnamon syrup, absinthe and bitters. Fill with ice, shake and strain into a double rocks glass or small tiki mug filled with ice. Garnish with a healthy bouquet of mint, the 3 cherries on a cocktail pick and freshly grated cinnamon.

bartender's tip: When it comes to Jamaican rum, I prefer to use Appleton 12 Year. As for Puerto Rican, using Bacardi 8 Year or Ron del Barrilito will do. For the overproof demerara rum, I suggest using Lemon Hart 151 or Hamilton 151. Pernod is a classic when it comes to absinthe in cocktails, but I also love St. George Absinthe Verte that is produced in California. Making falernum at home is great, but John D. Taylor's Velvet Falernum should be a staple in your home bar for making tiki drinks.

army & navy

The Army & Navy is a fantastic citrusy gin cocktail. I first stumbled upon this recipe while reading The Fine Art of Mixing Drinks, *by David Embury, many years ago at the start of my cocktail bartending career. This midcentury cocktail book is a must-read for any aspiring bartender and I always recommend it to anyone I'm training or anyone looking to get a better insight into making drinks. This drink is a sweeter variation on the Gin Sour and calls for orgeat instead of simple syrup. The orgeat adds a lovely nutty and aromatic note to this cocktail, making it more sultry while still remaining simple. This is a perfect cocktail for someone just getting into gin but wanting to try something a little different or for the gin lover with a sweet tooth.*

Makes 1 serving

2 oz (60 ml) gin
¾ oz (22 ml) fresh lemon juice
¾ oz (22 ml) Orgeat (page 184)
Luxardo cherry, for garnish
2 dashes of Angostura bitters, for garnish

In a cocktail shaker, combine the gin, lemon juice and orgeat. Fill with ice, shake vigorously and strain into a coupe glass. Garnish by dropping one Luxardo cherry into the bottom of the glass and add the bitters on top.

bartender's tip: Orgeat is pretty viscous, so shaking hard will yield a decent head on top of the cocktail, similar to using egg whites. I use a dropper to be more precise when adding my bitters and then pull a toothpick through it to make a design.

navy grog

The word grog originally referred to rum mixed with water that was rationed to crews of the British Royal Navy in 1740. It was later mixed with honey, molasses, lemon and cinnamon, and until the 1800s, a grog was usually served warm. Technological advances involving ice led to the drink being consumed cold as well. In 1941, Donn Beach started serving his own version of the Navy Grog in his tiki bar, Don the Beachcomber. This drink is considered to be part in what is called the holy trinity of tiki cocktails, alongside the Mai Tai and the Zombie.

Makes 1 serving

1 oz (30 ml) demerara rum

½ oz (15 ml) Puerto Rican rum

½ oz (15 ml) Jamaican rum

⅜ oz (11 ml) fresh lime juice

⅜ oz (11 ml) fresh grapefruit juice

½ oz (15 ml) Honey Syrup (page 179)

1 ice cone, for garnish (see tips)

Lime wheel, for garnish

3 Luxardo cherries, for garnish

Orchid, for garnish

In a cocktail shaker, combine the rums, lime juice, grapefruit juice and honey syrup. Fill with ice, shake and strain into a double rocks glass over an ice cone. Garnish with the lime wheel, cherries and orchid.

bartender's tips: For the demerara rum, try El Dorado 5 Year. And for something a little stronger, I love using Plantation O.F.T.D. Overproof instead of regular Jamaican rum. When using edible flowers, make sure you buy pesticide-free. Find a food-focused purveyor to ensure it is safe for using in food and cocktails.

Beachbum Berry makes a navy grog ice cone kit with Cocktail Kingdom. They have recreated the metal mold used to make cone ice just like tiki bartenders used during tiki's 1940–60s heyday.

"barnum was right"

The name of this drink is supposedly a reference to the saying "A sucker is born every minute," which is attributed to P. T. Barnum, an American showman of the mid-nineteenth century. This cocktail is fruity, refreshing and wonderfully zesty, a great choice to make if you're in the mood for something with gin that is sweet and aromatic. It's a very simple drink that will certainly sneak up on you, since the amount of booze outweighs the amount of citrus in the drink. I first came across this recipe in the 1941 Crosby Gaige's Cocktail Guide and Ladies' Companion, but was pleasantly surprised to see it also included in Trader Vic's Bartender's Guide, published in 1947.

Makes 1 serving

1½ oz (44 ml) gin
½ oz (15 ml) fresh lemon juice
1 oz (30 ml) apricot brandy
2 dashes of Angostura bitters
Long lemon twist (see tip), for garnish

In a cocktail shaker, combine the gin, lemon juice, apricot brandy and bitters. Fill with ice and shake vigorously. Strain into a coupe glass. Express the oils from the twist on top of the drink by squeezing it in half and then sliding it around the rim of your glass. To create the twist, twirl the lemon peel around with your fingers and it should hold its curled shape. Then, place the twist in the drink.

bartender's tip: Use a citrus peeler to make a long citrus twist. Try to cut the twist with as little white pith as possible to avoid adding a bitter element to your drinks.

hawaiian room

The Hawaiian Room was an oasis in the basement of New York's Lexington Hotel that showcased Hawaiian entertainment, South Seas decor and Polynesian food and drinks from 1937 to 1966. Its namesake cocktail, the Hawaiian Room, was invented sometime in the 1940s and is the only classic tropical cocktail, to my knowledge, made with Laird's Bonded Apple Brandy. Laird's has been making brandy in my home state of New Jersey since 1698, so this drink has always been pretty close to my heart. The Hawaiian Room is luscious and fruity, and combines interesting yet simple flavors. I love to serve it as a fall alternative to the pineapple daiquiri.

Makes 1 serving

1 oz (30 ml) white rum

½ oz (15 ml) Laird's Bonded Apple Brandy

½ oz (15 ml) Cointreau

¾ oz (22 ml) fresh pineapple juice

½ oz (15 ml) fresh lemon juice

¼ oz (7 ml) Demerara Syrup (page 180)

Long lemon twist, for garnish

Orchid, for garnish (optional)

In a cocktail shaker, combine the rum, apple brandy, Cointreau, pineapple juice, lemon juice and demerara syrup. Fill with ice, shake and strain into a coupe glass. Express the oils from the twist on top of the cocktail and discard the twist. Garnish with the orchid, if desired.

bronco buster

This is a delicious but deceivingly strong drink, perfect to get any cocktail party started. I love the way in which the spiciness of rye whiskey blends with the fruity notes of apple brandy. I highly suggest using Laird's Bonded Apple Brandy in this cocktail, instead of regular old 80-proof applejack. Hundred-proof apple brandy really is the best choice; the lighter flavor of applejack doesn't assert a strong enough apple flavor against the rest of the bright notes in this drink. This is a great option for a whiskey lover who usually drinks more spirit-forward drinks but might be in the mood for something with a little bit of citrus. Ted Saucier didn't have much to say about this drink when he documented it in his book Bottoms Up! *in 1951. In my opinion, this drink deserves a little more attention. You'll thank me when you're bustin' broncos all night long!*

Makes 1 serving

1 oz (30 ml) rye whiskey
1 oz (30 ml) Laird's Bonded Apple Brandy
¾ oz (22 ml) fresh lemon juice
¾ oz (22 ml) orange curaçao or triple sec
Long orange twist, for garnish

In a cocktail shaker, combine the rye whiskey, apple brandy, lemon juice and curaçao. Fill with ice and shake. Strain into a double rocks glass over ice. Express the oils from the twist on top of the drink by squeezing it in half and sliding it around the rim of your glass. Then, place the twist in the drink.

bartender's tip: If you decide to use triple sec or Cointreau instead of an orange curaçao, such as Grand Marnier or Pierre Ferrand, you might want to add a bar spoon of simple syrup just to sweeten it up a bit. Triple secs tend to be much drier than orange curaçao.

dama de la noche crusta

This is a luscious and exotic drink with origins from Medellín, Colombia. The name "Dama de la Noche" translates to "Lady of the Evening," but the reference is to a Philippine tropical tree whose blooms emit an intoxicating fragrance only at nightfall, so breathtakingly beautiful it almost puts you in a trance. There's no Dama de la Noche perfume in the drink, however; it is, in fact, delicious, floral and highly aromatic because of the use of orange flower water.

Makes 1 serving

Dash of orange flower water
Sugar, for rimming
1 ½ oz (44 ml) cognac
½ oz (15 ml) curaçao
2 dashes of Angostura bitters
1 oz (30 ml) fresh pineapple juice
½ oz (15 ml) fresh lime juice
Orange peel, for orange floret (optional)
Cocktail pick, for orange floret (optional)

Rim your coupe glass with sugar by dipping the edge of the glass in the orange flower water and then dipping it into the sugar. In a cocktail shaker, combine the cognac, curaçao, bitters, pineapple juice and lime juice. Fill with ice and shake. Strain into your sugar-rimmed glass. To make an orange floret garnish, make a very long orange peel and then roll it up so it resembles a rose and secure it with the cocktail pick. Garnish with the orange blossom, if desired.

pisco apricot tropicáls

This drink was most definitely inspired by another classic drink called the Pisco Punch and first appeared in Charles H. Baker's The South American Gentleman's Companion *in 1951. It was made for Baker at the Lima Country Club in Peru. If you're not familiar with it, Pisco is a type of brandy produced in winemaking regions of Peru and Chile. It is made by distilling fermented grape juice into a high-proof spirit. I've included my adapted recipe, but others have also made amendments to the recipe by replacing the pineapple juice with pineapple syrup. Using pineapple syrup will yield a much sweeter drink, so I will leave it up to your preference. I think it is a delightful and fruity drink as is when made with fresh pineapple juice, but if you feel like being adventurous, I've included the recipe for Pineapple Syrup on page 182, just in case.*

Makes 1 serving

1½ oz (44 ml) Pisco
½ oz (15 ml) apricot liqueur
½ oz (15 ml) fresh lime juice
1 oz (30 ml) fresh pineapple juice
2 dashes of Angostura bitters
Fresh pineapple wedge, for garnish

In a cocktail shaker, combine the Pisco, apricot liqueur, lime juice, pineapple juice and bitters. Fill with ice, shake and strain into a coupe glass. I like to garnish mine with a small pineapple wedge.

bartender's tip: If you're making the pineapple syrup version of this cocktail, adjust the recipe by using ¾ ounce (22 ml) of fresh lime juice and ¾ ounce (22 ml) of pineapple syrup to maintain a balanced cocktail.

stirred & boozy

Prohibition, followed by the Great Depression and World War II, left Americans needing a good stiff drink. From bustling cities to new suburbs, high-quality liquor was flowing freely. The immortal words of James Bond, "shaken, not stirred," will forever be entwined with the swinging 1960s and the vodka martini, but it is simply not the case here.

A stirred, or "clear," drink is any that contains predominantly or all alcohol. These drinks are considered sipping drinks because they are spirit forward and are meant to be consumed at a slower rate. Stirred drinks are heavy and silky smooth on the tongue and should contain no hints of bubbles or aeration, aka we do not shake these. When thinking about stirred drinks of the midcentury, a Manhattan or an old-fashioned might come to mind as well. These were popular cocktails of the time but, in fact, predate this time period. In this chapter, I'm going over variations on those cocktails that bartenders of the midcentury re-created as their own.

When making stirred cocktails, combine all your ingredients, except garnishes, in a mixing glass and then fill the glass with ice. To stir, keep the back of your bar spoon touching the inside of the glass and use your fingers to spin the spoon around. Your wrist should not be moving; this may take some practice. The idea is to have very little room between the ice and the glass and to be gently twirling your spoon so that the drink does not become aerated and maintains its silky texture.

Tools of the Trade

To make the drinks in this chapter, you will need a mixing glass, a julep strainer, a bar spoon, a jigger and a citrus peeler. The glassware needed is a coupe glass, a single old-fashioned glass and a double old-fashioned glass.

sherry darling

This is a drink I made for the 2014 winter menu during my time at Dutch Kills in Long Island City, New York. It looks like a simple drink, but it has so much flavor and depth. Pedro Ximénez is rich and full-bodied and has flavors of raisins, figs, roasted nuts and spices. Its sweetness stands up to the high-proof (100-proof) apple brandy, and the mezcal dries this drink out slightly and adds a lovely smoky finish.

Makes 1 serving

1 ¾ oz (52 ml) Laird's Bonded Apple Brandy
¾ oz (22 ml) Pedro Ximénez sherry
½ oz (15 ml) mezcal
Long lemon twist, for garnish

If you have a large-format cube of ice, you can build this drink in a glass, then add your large cube and stir 5 or 6 times. If not, in a mixing glass, combine the apple brandy, the sherry and the mezcal with ice, stir and strain over ice into a double old-fashioned glass. Express the oils from the twist on top of the drink by squeezing it in half and then slide it around the rim of your glass. Then, place the twist in the drink.

townes van zandt

When I created this drink, I was inspired by a martini called the Van Zandt, which is a mixture of gin, dry vermouth and apricot liqueur. I made it instead with rye whiskey, peach liqueur and bitters for a perfect summer Manhattan variation. The Manhattan, a cocktail that was created decades before the midcentury, was at the height of its popularity during this time. This drink is much drier than a classic Manhattan because of the use of dry vermouth instead of sweet, which allows the sweetness and fruitiness of the peach liqueur to really shine through. I decided to keep the name of the original cocktail that I drew inspiration from and added "Townes" in reference to one of my favorite musicians.

Makes 1 serving

2 oz (60 ml) rye whiskey
¾ oz (22 ml) dry vermouth
¼ oz (7 ml) peach liqueur
2 dashes of Angostura bitters
Long lemon twist, for garnish

In a mixing glass, combine the rye whiskey, vermouth, peach liqueur and bitters with ice, stir and strain into a coupe glass. Express the oils from the twist by squeezing it in half on top of the drink and then slide it around the rim of your glass. Then, place the twist in the drink.

monte carlo

If you're a fan of an old-fashioned (bourbon, sugar and bitters), then this Bénédictine-spiked old-fashioned variation from The Fine Art of Mixing Drinks, *by David Embury, circa 1948, just might be for you. This is one of my go-to drinks to serve when a guest at my bar loves an old-fashioned but wants to try something different. Rye is drier and much spicier than the usual bourbon, and Bénédictine adds a slightly sweet and herbal note to help balance it out.*

Makes 1 serving

2¼ oz (67 ml) rye whiskey
½ oz (15 ml) Bénédictine
3 dashes of Angostura bitters
Long lemon twist, for garnish

If you have a large-format cube of ice, you can build this drink in an old-fashioned glass, then add your large cube and stir 5 or 6 times. If not, in a mixing glass, combine the rye whiskey, Bénédictine and bitters with ice, stir and strain over ice into an old-fashioned glass. Express the oils from the twist on top of the drink by squeezing it in half and then slide it around the rim of your glass. Then, place the twist in the drink.

arsenic &
old lace

This cocktail has appeared in various books over the years under different names
(Attention Cocktail or the Atty), but it appears as the Arsenic & Old Lace in Crosby
Gaige's Cocktail Guide and Ladies' Companion, written in 1941. Arsenic and Old
Lace is a comedy by American playwright Joseph Kesselring, written in 1939. It became
best known for its film adaptation starring Cary Grant and directed by Frank Capra. It
was also the inspiration for my blog name because it is one of my favorite gin martini
variations. At the first sight of spring, I want to drink a crisp and floral cocktail and this
one definitely fits the bill!

Makes 1 serving

2 oz (60 ml) gin

¾ oz (22 ml) dry vermouth

¼ oz (7 ml) crème de violette

Absinthe rinse

Long orange twist, for garnish

In a mixing glass, combine the gin, vermouth and crème de violette with ice
and stir. Rinse a coupe glass with absinthe. You can do this by pouring a tiny bit
of absinthe into the glass, swirling it to coat the glass and then discarding the
absinthe. Strain your cocktail into the absinthe-rinsed glass. Express the oils from
the twist by squeezing it in half on top of the drink and then slide it around the rim
of your glass. Then, place the twist in the drink.

bartender's tips: A very popular violette liqueur is Rothman & Winter's,
but another great option is the Giffard's. I am constantly using St. George Absinthe
Verte, but you can use a classic standby, such as Pernod. Alternatively, for the
garnish, you can express the twist and discard it, then garnish the drink with edible
flowers.

battle of
new orleans

This drink is named after the final battle of the War of 1812 where General Andrew Jackson faced off against British general Edward Pakenham, and admiral Alexander Cochrane. The actual fighting lasted barely thirty minutes and it will take you even less time to make this cocktail, a Sazerac-meets-old-fashioned variation from the 1941 Crosby Gaige's Cocktail Guide and Ladies' Companion.

Makes 1 serving

2½ oz (74 ml) bourbon
¼ oz (7 ml) Simple Syrup (page 179)
2 dashes of Peychaud's bitters
Dash of absinthe
Dash of orange bitters
Long lemon twist, for garnish

If you have a large-format cube of ice, you can build this drink in a glass, then add your large cube and stir 5 or 6 times. If not, in a mixing glass, combine the bourbon, simple syrup, Peychaud's bitters, absinthe and orange bitters with ice, stir and strain over ice into a double old-fashioned glass. Express the oils from the twist on top of the drink by squeezing it in half and then slide it around the rim of your glass. Then, place the twist in the drink.

don't give up the ship

Adapted from Trader Vic's Bartender's Guide, *published in 1947. This is an unusual and herbaceous martini-esque cocktail. It was named after Captain James Lawrence's stoic final order as he lay dying aboard his ship the USS* Chesapeake: *"Don't give up the ship. Fight her till she sinks." This became the rallying cry for the fledging U.S. Navy, which ultimately overpowered the British and won the War of 1812. What all this has to do with gin and Fernet-Branca is anyone's guess, but it's a bitter, herbal and aromatic cocktail that makes one hell of an after-dinner drink.*

Makes 1 serving

1½ oz (44 ml) gin
½ oz (15 ml) Fernet-Branca
½ oz (15 ml) sweet vermouth
½ oz (15 ml) curaçao
Long orange twist, for garnish

In a mixing glass, combine the gin, Fernet-Branca, vermouth and curaçao with ice, stir and strain into a coupe glass. Express the oils from the twist on top of the drink by squeezing it in half and then slide it around the rim of your glass. Then, place the twist in the drink.

talent scout

This is another very easy old-fashioned variation from Bottom's Up! *by Ted Saucier, published in 1951. This is slightly sweeter and fruitier than your average old-fashioned because of the use of curaçao. It's a great option for someone that still wants a stiff drink but is looking for something a little more light and crisp. I love serving these to my die-hard old-fashioned drinkers in the summer months.*

Makes 1 serving

2½ oz (74 ml) bourbon
½ oz (15 ml) curaçao
2 dashes of Angostura bitters
Long lemon twist, for garnish

If you have a large-format cube of ice, you can build this drink in an old-fashioned glass, then add your large cube and stir 5 or 6 times. If not, in a mixing glass, combine the bourbon, curaçao and bitters with ice, stir and strain over ice into an old-fashioned glass. Express the oils from the twist on top of the drink by squeezing it in half and then slide it around the rim of your glass. Then, place the twist in the drink.

astoria

Originally from the old Waldorf Astoria hotel in New York City. I first found this cocktail while skimming through Bottoms Up! by Ted Saucier, published in 1951. I love a vermouth-heavy martini, but this recipe called for 2:1 vermouth to gin, which is basically a reversed martini. Let's meet in the middle and make it a 50/50 martini, which is by far my favorite ratio. A splash of orange bitters makes this martini variation much more citrusy and bright. This drink is delicious if you're using a London dry gin, but if you want to make it really special, I suggest using an Old Tom gin. Old Tom is a sweeter, rounder style of gin and works marvelously to balance out the large amount of dry vermouth in this cocktail.

Makes 1 serving

1½ oz (44 ml) gin
1½ oz (44 ml) dry vermouth
2 dashes of orange bitters
Long lemon twist, for garnish

In a mixing glass, combine the gin, vermouth and bitters with ice, stir and strain into a coupe glass. Express the oils from the twist by squeezing it in half on top of the drink and then slide it around the rim of your glass. Then, place the twist in the drink.

good fellow

Some of the best drinks, in my opinion, happen to only have three ingredients. This drink is no exception. It is simple but full of flavor. Bénédictine is a French herbal liqueur flavored with some 27 flowers, berries, herbs, roots and spices. It adds so much flavor and aromatics to this drink alongside the Angostura bitters and vanilla notes of the cognac. This is a cognac old-fashioned variation from Trader Vic, circa 1947.

Makes 1 serving

2 ¼ oz (67 ml) cognac
½ oz (15 ml) Bénédictine
2 dashes of Angostura bitters
Long lemon twist, for garnish

If you have a large-format cube of ice, you can build this drink in an old-fashioned glass, then add your large cube and stir 5 or 6 times. If not, in a mixing glass, combine the cognac, Bénédictine and bitters with ice, stir and strain over ice into an old-fashioned glass. Express the oils from the twist on top of the drink by squeezing it in half and then slide it around the rim of your glass. Then, place the twist in the drink.

arawak

I'm constantly grabbing my 1947 edition of Trader Vic's Bartender's Guide *for inspiration. This cocktail reminds me of a Manhattan, except it's sweeter and made with rum and sherry instead of rye and sweet vermouth. The ingredients and name also make an interesting historical reference. The Arawak were indigenous peoples of the West Indies who Christopher Columbus came upon on his 1492 voyage. The parts are all there, with Caribbean rum and bitters mixed with a Spanish fortified wine. I'm sure Columbus didn't leave Spain without a ship stocked to the brim with sherry. I know I wouldn't! This cocktail is rich, sweet and smooth, and has a little bit of funk when using the right Jamaican rum. One of my favorite go-to after-dinner drinks.*

Makes 1 serving

2 oz (60 ml) Jamaican rum

1 oz (30 ml) Pedro Ximénez sherry

Dash of Angostura bitters

Long lemon twist, for garnish

In a mixing glass, combine the rum, sherry and bitters with ice, stir and strain into a coupe glass. Express the oils from the twist by squeezing it in half on top of the drink and then slide it around the rim of your glass. Then, place the twist in the drink.

bartender's tip: My standby Jamaican rum is Appleton 12 Year and it is a great option for using in this cocktail. However, if you wanted a less sweet drink and something a bit stiffer, using a rum such as Smith & Cross is a great idea. Smith & Cross is a navy-strength rum (114 proof) and has something called "rancio" ethers, which gives it a very funky flavor profile.

gloria

If a Negroni is too bitter, too sweet, or too aggressive for your palate, then this is a great drink to test the waters with. It's much drier and a tad bit fruitier from the use of Cointreau and dry vermouth instead of just the sweet vermouth used in a classic Negroni. It's also a lot less bitter because a smaller amount of Campari is used in this recipe. The Gloria is a fantastic cocktail to serve to someone who likes a Negroni but is looking to try something a little different, or for those who like things a little less sweet. It's a favorite of mine to make when the weather is warmer but I still need something strong to do the trick. This drink is a cross between a martini and a Negroni, and is found in Trader Vic's Bartender's Guide, *published in 1947.*

Makes 1 serving

1½ oz (44 ml) gin

½ oz (15 ml) dry vermouth

½ oz (15 ml) Cointreau

½ oz (15 ml) Campari

Long orange twist, for garnish

In a mixing glass, combine the gin, vermouth, Cointreau and Campari with ice, stir and strain into a coupe glass. Express the oils from the twist on top of the drink by squeezing it in half and then slide it around the rim of your glass. Then, place the twist in the drink.

moonraker #1

This is a delightful cognac drink that is perfect to serve in the warmer months, especially around the time when the winter weather breaks and we are getting our first glimpses of spring. Lillet Blanc has a light, crisp, citrusy aroma with a mild sweetness that pairs perfectly with the fruitiness of peach liqueur, warming vanilla notes of cognac and just a touch of anise from the absinthe. For a darker and spicier version of this drink, swap out the Lillet Blanc for Dubonnet Red. Adapted from the 1947 Trader Vic's Bartender's Guide.

Makes 1 serving

2 oz (60 ml) cognac
½ oz (15 ml) peach liqueur
½ oz (15 ml) Lillet Blanc
Absinthe rinse
Long lemon twist, for garnish

In a mixing glass, combine the cognac, peach liqueur and Lillet Blanc with ice and stir. Rinse a coupe glass with absinthe. You can do this by pouring a tiny bit of absinthe into the glass, swirling it to coat the glass and then discarding the absinthe. Pour your cocktail into the absinthe-rinsed glass. Express the oils from the twist on top of the drink by squeezing it in half and then slide it around the rim of your glass. Then, place the twist in the drink.

bartender's tip: If you find yourself gravitating toward making a few absinthe-rinsed drinks I suggest buying a small atomizer and filling it with absinthe. Then, you would simply give your glass a few sprays and it wouldn't lead to any wasted absinthe.

long &
fizzy

We've come a long way since the Tom and John Collins days, which were popular standby drinks of the midcentury. In David Embury's 1948 *The Fine Art of Mixing Drinks,* he describes the Collins as "a lemonade made with charged water and spiked with gin or some other liquor." Although a Collins-style drink can still remain simple, the way it was intended, it's still great to explore other variations of this drink. Some are simple, such as the Southside Special, a Jamaican rum cooler, and others more complicated, such as the Colonel Beach's Plantation Punch (page 86) with a whopping ten ingredients, but all the drinks that you'll find in this chapter are fizzy, refreshing and totally worth making. The queen cocktail of this era is undoubtedly the Moscow Mule (page 77), which was created in the 1940s and became a cultural phenomenon inspiring the iconic copper mug and cocktail parties dubbed "Mule Parties."

A Collins is basically a sour cocktail consisting of a base spirit, juice, simple syrup and carbonated water. It is shaken and served long, meaning in a Collins or highball glass and topped with soda water. Collins glasses are tall, round and usually have a 12- to 16-ounce (355- to 475-ml) capacity. They are a great option when you want a lighter cocktail with a bit more dilution. Since the water content is higher in this style of beverage and it also sits on ice, a good five-second shake is all that is needed before straining over ice.

Tools of the Trade

To make the drinks in this chapter, you will need a cocktail shaker, a Hawthorne strainer, a jigger and good-quality sparkling water. The glassware needed is a Collins or highball glass.

after midnight

This is my own spin on another Collins in this chapter, the Stay Up Late (page 81). The name is a nod to—you guessed it—staying up after midnight, but also to a Patsy Cline song of the same name. I love the way apple brandy and mezcal go together. The apple brandy is hot, spicy and full of apple flavor, baking spices and oaky vanilla. The way the smoky flavors of the mezcal blend with the apple brandy give it a smoke-in-the-orchard type of vibe. It makes a great fall or winter highball option, but can be enjoyed all year long.

Makes 1 serving

1 oz (30 ml) mezcal

1 oz (30 ml) Laird's Bonded Apple Brandy

¾ oz (22 ml) fresh lemon juice

¾ oz (22 ml) Simple Syrup (page 179)

Sparkling water

Apple fan (see tip), for garnish

Cocktail pick, for skewering the apples

In a cocktail shaker, combine the mezcal, apple brandy, lemon juice and simple syrup and shake with ice. Strain into a highball glass over ice and top with sparkling water. Garnish with the apple fan.

bartender's tip: To make an apple fan, stack 3 apple slices together and then fan them out. Secure the shape by sticking a cocktail pick at the end of the apples where they all meet.

mai tai spritz

The one thing I love, especially in the summertime, is indulging in a perfectly made Mai Tai. The trouble is that it can get a little dangerous. I created this drink to be a lower ABV (alcohol by volume) version of a classic Mai Tai, so you don't have to feel guilty about having a few. This is a great drink to make when it's hot and you're craving something tropical but don't want to feel the boozy effects of a strong tiki drink.

Makes 1 serving

1 oz (30 ml) dark rum
½ oz (15 ml) dry curaçao
½ oz (15 ml) fresh lime juice
½ oz (15 ml) Orgeat (page 184)
Sparkling wine or water
Mint sprig, for garnish
Luxardo cherry, for garnish
Powdered sugar, for garnish

In a cocktail shaker, combine the rum, curaçao, lime juice and orgeat and shake with ice. Strain into a large snifter over crushed ice and top with sparkling wine. Garnish with the mint sprig and cherry, and dust with powdered sugar.

bartender's tip: Spirit recommendations for this drink are Plantation Original Dark Rum and Pierre Ferrand Dry Curaçao. For the wine, a good crisp and full-bodied sparkling brut, such as Gruet, will suffice.

roman holiday

Negroni lovers, rejoice! I took my two favorite ingredients in the classic Negroni (gin and Campari—duh!) and combined them with refreshing and fruity flavors to make the perfect summer drink. This drink has a slightly lower ABV because I use a lower-ABV bitter (the Campari). Using fresh pineapple juice and ginger syrup make this drink light, super-refreshing and slightly tropical. One can only hope that with a few sips, it will transport you on your very own Roman holiday.

Makes 1 serving

1 oz (30 ml) gin

1 oz (30 ml) Campari

1 oz (30 ml) fresh pineapple juice

½ oz (15 ml) fresh lemon juice

¾ oz (22 ml) Ginger Syrup (page 180)

Sparkling water

Fresh pineapple wedge, for garnish

Pineapple leaves, for garnish

In a cocktail shaker, combine the gin, Campari, pineapple juice, lemon juice and ginger syrup and shake with ice. Strain into a highball glass over ice and top with sparkling water. Garnish with the pineapple wedge and pineapple leaves.

moscow mule

Created in the early 1940s, a Moscow Mule features vodka, ginger beer and lime. There is some dispute over the exact origins of this drink, but accounts credit a meeting between John G. Martin, an executive at the company that bottled the then very unknown Smirnoff vodka, and Jack Morgan, owner of the Cock 'n' Bull bar in Hollywood and a ginger beer producer. Together they created an easy-to-make drink using their underperforming products and gave it a catchy name ("Moscow" in reference to vodka's Russian roots) for marketing. After a break during World War II, growing interest in Hollywood resumed and ads for "Mule Parties" featuring celebrities helped raise the popularity of this beverage and that of vodka, which would go on to be the most popular spirit in the United States. Traditionally, this drink is served in copper mugs (myths contend that another friend made copper products), but a highball or Collins glass are suitable options for serving, too. I like to use fresh ginger instead of premade ginger beer for a spicier and refreshing alternative.

Makes 1 serving

2 oz (60 ml) vodka
¾ oz (22 ml) Ginger Syrup (page 180)
½ oz (15 ml) fresh lime juice
Sparkling water
Candied ginger, for garnish
Cocktail pick, for skewering ginger

In a cocktail shaker, combine the vodka, ginger syrup and lime juice with ice and shake. Strain into a copper mug or highball glass over ice and top with sparkling water. Garnish with a piece of candied ginger on a cocktail pick.

suffering bastard

Invented in 1942 by the legendary globetrotting barman Joe Scialom at Shepheard's Hotel in Cairo, Egypt, this drink was originally called the "Suffering Bar Steward." Try saying that fast and you'll see where the drink got its name. I first saw this recipe in Jeff Berry's 2009 Beachbum Berry Remixed *and this recipe was adapted at PKNY in New York City. This a boozy highball that is citrusy and slightly spicy from ginger, with a hint of aromatics from the use of bitters. Another great way to have this drink is by swapping out the cognac for bourbon.*

Makes 1 serving

1 oz (30 ml) cognac
1 oz (30 ml) gin
1 oz (30 ml) fresh lime juice
½ oz (15 ml) Simple Syrup (page 179)
½ oz (15 ml) Ginger Syrup (page 180)
2 dashes of Angostura bitters
Sparkling water
Cocktail pick, for skewering garnishes
Orange slice, for garnish
Cucumber slices, for garnish
Candied ginger, for garnish
Mint sprig, for garnish

In a cocktail shaker, combine the cognac, gin, lime juice, simple syrup, ginger syrup and bitters and shake with ice. Strain into a highball glass over ice, top with sparkling water and, using a cocktail pick, garnish with the orange slice, cucumber slices, candied ginger and mint sprig.

stay up late

This is truly one of my favorite cocktails of all time. The only thing that makes this different from the original Tom Collins is the addition of cognac. Although slight, the cognac adds oaky vanilla depth and flavor. Oftentimes, I do wind up staying up late after having a few of these. This is a simple Tom Collins variation from The Stork Club Bar Book, *published in 1946.*

Makes 1 serving

1½ oz (44 ml) gin

½ oz (15 ml) cognac

¾ oz (22 ml) fresh lemon juice

¾ oz (22 ml) Simple Syrup (page 179)

Sparkling water

Orange slice, for garnish

Luxardo cherry, for garnish

In a cocktail shaker, combine the gin, cognac, lemon juice and simple syrup and shake with ice. Strain into a highball glass over ice, top with sparkling water and garnish with the orange slice and cherry.

sidewinder's fang

The "fang" here must come from the tart bite of the lime and passion fruit, but together with the sweetness of dark rums, they balance each other out. This is possibly the only highball drink I know that includes passion fruit and is a really great example of a tropical cocktail coming together with more classic style influences. It is like a sweet effervescent piece of candy, so beware—it could get dangerous! This 1960s cocktail originates from the Lanai restaurant in San Mateo, California. On the Lanai's menu, this drink was described as "the banisher of troubles" and I must agree that it certainly does the trick!

Makes 1 serving

Long orange peel, for garnish
1 oz (30 ml) demerara rum
1 oz (30 ml) dark Jamaican rum
1½ oz (44 ml) fresh orange juice
½ oz (15 ml) fresh lime juice
½ oz (15 ml) Passion Fruit Syrup (page 184)
Sparkling water
Mint sprig, for garnish

Line your glass with the Sidewinder's Fang—the long orange peel—with one end hanging over the rim of the glass. Fill the glass with ice to hold the peel in place.

In a cocktail shaker, combine the rums, orange juice, lime juice and passion fruit syrup and shake with ice. Strain into your ice-filled glass, top with sparkling water and finish it with a sprig of mint.

new orleans buck

This is a spectacular Mule or Rum Buck variation that is refreshing and juicy. Originally from Jones' Complete Barguide, *by Stan Jones, it first called for the use of orange juice, but my favorite way to make and indulge in this drink is to replace the orange juice with pineapple juice, which makes this cocktail much more flavorful and tropical and a little bit more interesting. The substitution of pineapple juice comes from an adapted recipe by Christy Pope of Milk & Honey in New York City, circa 2004.*

Makes 1 serving

2 oz (60 ml) aged rum
1 oz (30 ml) fresh pineapple juice
½ oz (15 ml) fresh lime juice
½ oz (15 ml) Ginger Syrup (page 180)
2 dashes of Angostura bitters
Sparkling water
Orange wedge, for garnish
Candied ginger, for garnish
Cocktail pick, for skewering garnishes

In a cocktail shaker, combine the rum, pineapple juice, lime juice, ginger syrup and bitters and shake with ice. Strain into a highball glass over ice and top with sparkling water. Garnish with the orange wedge and candied ginger on a cocktail pick.

colonel beach's plantation punch

This is a refreshing and fruity rum punch that is great for the summer months. It has a combination of three different styles of rums, a technique that Don the Beachcomber used frequently in his recipes to add unique flavors to his drinks. I adapted the recipe to call for ginger syrup and club soda instead of ginger beer. Making Ginger Syrup (page 180) from freshly pressed ginger juice yields a spicier and more flavorful beverage. Don the Beachcomber served this drink at his Colonel's Plantation Beefsteak House in Hawaii in the 1950s. This drink was also included in Beachbum Berry Remixed, *by Jeff Berry, published in 2009.*

Makes 1 serving

1 oz (30 ml) dark Jamaican rum

½ oz (15 ml) Puerto Rican rum

½ oz (15 ml) Barbados rum

¼ oz (7 ml) falernum

1 oz (30 ml) fresh pineapple juice

½ oz (15 ml) fresh lime juice

½ oz (15 ml) Ginger Syrup (page 180)

Dash of Angostura bitters

2 dashes of absinthe

Sparkling water

Fresh pineapple chunks, for garnish

Candied ginger, for garnish

Cocktail pick, for skewering garnishes

Mint sprig, for garnish (optional)

In a cocktail shaker, combine the rums, falernum, pineapple juice, lime juice, ginger syrup, bitters and absinthe and shake with ice. Strain into a highball glass or tiki mug over ice and top with sparkling water. Garnish with the pineapple chunks and candied ginger on a cocktail pick and add the mint sprig, if desired.

bartender's tip: Spirit recommendations for this drink are Hamilton Jamaican Pot Still Black Rum, Ron del Barrilito 3 Star Puerto Rican Rum and Plantation Barbados 5 Year Old Rum.

invisible gin

The fruity flavors of apricot and pineapple go beautifully with the botanicals of gin, while ginger syrup makes this cocktail refreshing and spicy. It's a little too good and easy to forget the strength of the booze. So, pace yourself! The Invisible Gin is one of my go-to cocktails to make on a hot summer day. This is a super-refreshing and fruity gin Collins variation adapted from The South American Gentleman's Companion, *by Charles H. Baker, circa 1951.*

Makes 1 serving

1½ oz (44 ml) gin
½ oz (15 ml) apricot liqueur
1 oz (30 ml) fresh pineapple juice
½ oz (15 ml) fresh lemon juice
½ oz (15 ml) Ginger Syrup (page 180)
Sparkling water
Fresh pineapple chunks, for garnish
Candied ginger, for garnish
Cocktail pick, for skewering garnishes

In a cocktail shaker, combine the gin, apricot liqueur, pineapple juice, lemon juice and ginger syrup and shake with ice. Strain into a highball glass over ice and top with sparkling water. Garnish with the pineapple chunks and candied ginger on a cocktail pick.

northside special

Not every drink needs to be complicated, and sometimes, using simple ingredients really lets the flavor of the spirit come through. That is certainly the case with the Northside Special, where simple and classic ingredients are paired with the delicious flavors of rum. In this drink, you can get creative by choosing different types of rum to accomplish varying flavor profiles. If you use a Jamaican rum, you will get a cocktail that has a bit more funk, whereas a black Bermuda rum will yield a sweeter and more molasses-forward flavor. Using either will deliver a tasty concoction worth savoring every citrusy sip.

Cocktail parties and mixing at home was a huge part of the drinking culture in the midcentury. If you're entertaining, it might be fun to set up a bar station and put out a few different rums of your choice and let your guests decide which one they'd like to mix with. This delicious and simple Jamaican cooler recipe is from The Fine Art of Mixing Drinks, by David Embury, published in 1948.

Makes 1 serving

2 oz (60 ml) dark Jamaican rum or Bermuda rum
1½ oz (44 ml) fresh orange juice
½ oz (15 ml) fresh lemon juice
½ oz (15 ml) Simple Syrup (page 179)
Sparkling water
Orange wedge, for garnish

In a cocktail shaker, combine the rum, orange juice, lemon juice and simple syrup and shake with ice. Strain into a highball glass over ice and top with sparkling water. Garnish with the orange wedge.

icy &
swizzled

There's nothing more reviving than sipping on a well-made cocktail chilled to the utmost perfection over crushed ice. From fixes to swizzles, these concoctions consist of a base spirit, citrus, sweetener and crushed ice. Although crushed ice drinks can be traced back to 1862 in *How to Mix Drinks* by Jerry Thomas, they were most likely a popular style of serving cocktails in the postwar midcentury landscape because of the rise of escapism and tropical drinks.

A fix is a sour-style cocktail served down over crushed ice. This style of drink has evolved over time to contain many types of citrus, fruit syrups or freshly muddled seasonal fruit. A fix-style drink is usually built in a cocktail shaker, dry shaken and then the undiluted cocktail is poured over crushed ice.

Swizzle-style cocktails have a bit more work involved. A swizzle is named after the way it's mixed, rather than for ingredients used. To prepare one, it is best to use an authentic swizzle stick. Real swizzle sticks are long stems snapped off a tree native to the Caribbean and feature multiple horizontal prongs at the end. When spun rapidly between both of your hands inside a cold cocktail, the stick should create a layer of frost on the outside of the glass—a sure sign that your drink is chilled to perfection.

Tools of the Trade

To make the drinks in this chapter, you will need a cocktail shaker, a jigger, a muddler and a swizzle stick. Crushed ice is of the utmost importance. The glassware needed is a snifter, a double rocks glass and an array of long glasses, such as Collins, highball or footed pilsner glasses and tiki mugs.

flying down to rio

The most important thing to me about tropical drinks is the way they transport you to another place, perhaps even another time. I based the Flying Down to Rio on the Painkiller—a cocktail that was invented in the 1970s by Daphne Henderson at the Soggy Dollar Bar in the British Virgin Islands. My version is a sweet and fruity drink made with a cachaça that has been aged in amburana wood, an indigenous wood found only in the forests of Latin America. The aging of this spirit offers warm, savory notes of allspice, cinnamon, vanilla and Thai basil, backed by earthy sugarcane, with a hint of toasted almond on the finish. All these flavors from the cachaça, combined with banana liqueur, fresh pineapple and orange juice and coconut cream make the Flying Down to Rio the perfect summer beverage. I wanted to pay homage to where the base spirit was from and I've always been a classic movie fan. What says escape to paradise more than a musical with Fred Astaire and Ginger Rogers in it? I promise this drink will surely make you want to dance the night away!

Makes 1 serving

1½ oz (44 ml) Avuá Amburana Cachaça
½ oz (15 ml) Giffard Banane du Brésil
1 oz (30 ml) fresh pineapple juice
½ oz (15 ml) fresh orange juice
¾ oz (22 ml) Coconut Cream (page 185)
Freshly grated nutmeg, for garnish
Pineapple leaves, for garnish
Cocktail umbrella, for garnish

In a cocktail shaker, combine the cachaça, Giffard Banane, pineapple juice, orange juice and coconut cream, dry shake (without ice) and then pour into a small glass, such as a snifter or double rocks glass, over crushed ice. Garnish with freshly grated nutmeg and pineapple leaves. A cocktail umbrella never hurt anyone either.

hamilton park
swizzle

I wouldn't say that Jersey City is a tropical paradise, but that didn't stop me from finding inspiration in one of my favorite parks and variating on the classic Queens Park Swizzle cocktail. I invented this drink during my time behind the bar at Lani Kai in 2010, a now-defunct New York City tropical bar owned by Julie Reiner. It was while working there that my love for tropical drinks, tiki and the midcentury really started to take shape. So, in some way, I owe a lot to that space and the people that I met and worked with during my time there. To make apple brandy slightly more "tiki," I infused it with mango tea. My only tweak to the original recipe is the addition of Angostura bitters.

Makes 1 serving

MANGO TEA–INFUSED APPLE BRANDY

4 oz (113 g) mango-flavored black loose-leaf tea

1 (750-ml) bottle apple brandy

COCKTAIL

1 oz (30 ml) mango tea–infused Laird's Apple Brandy

1 oz (30 ml) Palo Cortado sherry

¾ oz (22 ml) Pineapple Syrup (page 182)

¾ oz (22 ml) fresh lime juice

1 bar spoon falernum

5 dashes of Angostura bitters

Fresh pineapple slice, for garnish

Orchid, for garnish

To make the mango tea–infused apple brandy, add the mango-flavored black tea—I used SerendipiTea Magnificent Mango—to the bottle of apple brandy. Let steep for 1 hour. Strain into a clean bottle or decanter.

To make one cocktail, in a cocktail shaker, combine the mango tea–infused apple brandy, sherry, pineapple syrup, lime juice and falernum and dry shake (without ice). Pour into a Collins glass over crushed ice and swizzle. Float the bitters by dashing on top, then top with more crushed ice. Garnish with the pineapple slice and orchid.

the saguaro

I created this spring tequila swizzle that hits all the right notes. At first glance, this drink might appear sweet and fruity, but fear not. The Campari and yellow Chartreuse add lovely bitter and herbal flavors, while warm notes from the vanilla syrup and cardamom bitters round it out. I'd hate to compare it to a tart strawberry-rhubarb pie, but I'm going to. A boozy, delicious and complex one. This is a perfect cocktail to transition you from the late chill of spring and into the warm summer months. Although this is a new drink, I took flavor inspiration from crushed-ice drinks of the past and put a modern twist on it by using tequila.

Makes 1 serving

¾ oz (22 ml) fresh lemon juice
½ oz (15 ml) Vanilla Syrup (page 181)
2 strawberries, for muddling
Dash of cardamom bitters
Dash of rhubarb bitters
1½ oz (44 ml) tequila
½ oz (15 ml) Campari
½ oz (15 ml) yellow Chartreuse
Strawberry slice, for garnish
Pansy, for garnish
Freshly grated cinnamon, for garnish

In the bottom of a cocktail shaker, combine the lemon juice, vanilla syrup and 2 strawberries and muddle. Add the bitters, tequila, Campari and yellow Chartreuse, dry shake and then dump into a footed pilsner glass. Add crushed ice, swizzle and top with crushed ice again. Garnish with the strawberry slice, pansy and freshly grated cinnamon.

gringo honeymoon

A blend of two of my favorite spirits, mezcal and rum, this recipe makes for a spicy yet sweet and refreshing swizzle. This is my own variation on another drink called the Karaoke Honeymoon, which has spiced rum, made by a friend, Zack Genlaw-Rubin, with whom I worked at Dutch Kills. I really love the use of mezcal in this drink. Although there are sweeter flavors, it adds smokiness and slightly dries out and balances the rest of the ingredients. Using an overproof Jamaican rum, such as Smith & Cross, adds funky complex flavors and also strong boozy qualities. Faretti, which is a biscotti liqueur, provides a baking spice element that goes delightfully with the ginger, to give a gingersnap cookie effect to this drink. If Faretti is hard to come by, substituting amaretto will suffice. I wanted to keep the honeymoon reference, to pay my respects to the original drink, and thought "Gringo Honeymoon" a Robert Earl Keen song, was an appropriate fit considering the use of mezcal.

Makes 1 serving

1 oz (30 ml) mezcal

½ oz (15 ml) overproof Jamaican rum

½ oz (15 ml) Faretti biscotti liqueur or amaretto

½ oz (15 ml) fresh orange juice

½ oz (15 ml) fresh lemon juice

½ oz (15 ml) Ginger Syrup (page 180)

Orange wedge, for garnish

Freshly grated nutmeg, for garnish

In a cocktail shaker, combine the mezcal, rum, Faretti, orange juice, lemon juice and ginger syrup and dry shake. Pour into a highball glass with crushed ice and garnish with the orange wedge and freshly grated nutmeg.

mai tai

The Mai Tai is the quintessential tiki cocktail, as far as I'm concerned. It is one of the most classic and actually one of the most fought over. The founding fathers of tiki, Don the Beachcomber and Trader Vic, actually went to court over the rights to the drink, each claiming that he was the original creator. Vic won that battle and it is credited to him at Trader Vic's in Oakland, California, circa 1944. He claims that it got its name from a friend who was visiting from Tahiti. When she tried it for the first time, she declared "Maita'i roa," literally meaning "the very best!" or figuratively "out of this world!" The Mai Tai is a fairly tart and citrusy drink that is super-refreshing. Lime and rum dominate the flavor profile, while the curaçao and orgeat primarily add body and soften the drink.

Makes 1 serving

1 oz (30 ml) Martinique rhum

1 oz (30 ml) Jamaican rum

¾ oz (22 ml) fresh lime juice

⅜ oz (11 ml) curaçao

⅜ oz (11 ml) Orgeat (page 184)

Leafy mint sprig, for garnish

Lime wheel, for garnish

Orchid, for garnish

Powdered sugar, for garnish

In a cocktail shaker, combine the rums, lime juice, curaçao and orgeat, dry shake and pour into a Mai Tai glass over crushed ice. Garnish with a bouquet of mint, the lime wheel and orchid and a generous dusting of powdered sugar.

bartender's tip: For the Martinique rum, I suggest using Rhum Clément VSOP; and Appleton Estate for the Jamaican. Another twist to the base of this drink that I love doing is to use just 1½ ounces (44 ml) of Jamaican rum (omitting the Martinique rum) and then a ¼-ounce (7-ml) float of Hamilton 151 Overproof Demerara Rum on top.

1950 zombie

Don the Beachcomber tinkered with his recipes obsessively, changing them many times over the years. This is his revamped version of the original 1934 Zombie formula. I love the addition of pineapple juice and passion fruit, and the use of lighter rums in this drink. A much fruitier and less dangerous adaptation means you might be able to have more than just one.

Makes 1 serving

1 oz (30 ml) Puerto Rican rum

1 oz (30 ml) white rum

½ oz (15 ml) Hamilton 151 Overproof Demerara Rum

1 oz (30 ml) fresh pineapple juice

¼ oz (7 ml) fresh lime juice

½ oz (15 ml) Demerara Syrup (page 180)

1 bar spoon Passion Fruit Syrup (page 184)

2 dashes of Angostura bitters

Leafy mint sprig, for garnish

In a tiki mug, directly build the rums, pineapple juice, lime juice, demerara syrup, passion fruit syrup and bitters. Fill with crushed ice, swizzle and top with crushed ice again. Garnish with a healthy bouquet of mint.

fog cutter

The Fog Cutter is a classic tiki cocktail popularized by one of the founding fathers of tiki, Trader Vic. Its three-spirit base of rum, gin and brandy make it a heavy-set drink that's surprisingly sippable. Orange and lemon juice makes the drink citrusy and vibrant, and the sherry and orgeat round it out with nuttiness. This drink is famous for being served in a Fog Cutter mug as pictured here, but any tiki mug will do. From the 1946 edition of Trader Vic's Book of Food and Drink, "This is delicious but a triple threat. You can get pretty stinking on these, no fooling." Also from the 1972 edition of Trader Vic's Bartender's Guide, "Fog Cutter, hell. After two of these, you won't even see the stuff." Proceed with caution.

Makes 1 serving

1½ oz (44 ml) white rum

½ oz (15 ml) cognac

½ oz (15 ml) gin

1 oz (30 ml) fresh orange juice

½ oz (15 ml) fresh lemon juice

½ oz (15 ml) Orgeat (page 184)

½ oz (15 ml) Amontillado sherry

Mint sprig, for garnish

Orchid, for garnish

Orange peel, for orange floret

Cocktail pick, for orange floret

In a cocktail shaker, combine the rum, cognac, gin, orange juice, lemon juice and orgeat, dry shake and then pour into a Collins glass over crushed ice. Swizzle and float the Amontillado sherry by pouring it on top. Garnish with the mint sprig and orchid. To make the orange floret, cut a long orange peel and then roll it so that it looks like a flower. You can secure its shape by using a toothpick or cocktail pick, then add it beside the mint and orchid. Garnish elaborately and drink jubilantly.

night flight

I know, easy and tiki don't normally go together, but this cocktail features just three perfectly balanced ingredients. If you aren't familiar with rhum agricole, it's a style of rum traditionally distilled in the French Caribbean Islands, using sugarcane juice rather than molasses (the latter of which is the base for most other styles of rum). This method of distillation yields a funky, vegetal, grassy quality and adds so much flavor and depth to an otherwise sweet drink. Although this drink has tiki origins, it makes the perfect winter daiquiri substitute because of the rich flavor that the maple syrup adds. This is a very easy and delicious drink from the 1947 Trader Vic's Bartender's Guide.

Makes 1 serving

2 oz (60 ml) Martinique rhum
1 oz (30 ml) fresh lime juice
¾ oz (22 ml) pure maple syrup
Lime wheel, for garnish
Luxardo cherry, for garnish

In a cocktail shaker, combine the rhum, lime juice and maple syrup, dry shake and pour into a double rocks glass over crushed ice. Top with more crushed ice and garnish with the lime wheel and cherry.

bartender's tip: Let me note that not all maple syrups are created equal. You'll want to use a dark Grade A or Grade B maple syrup. Under no circumstances should you use anything maple flavored or that contains high-fructose corn syrup. Real maple syrup is made from the sap of a maple tree, which has been collected in the woods and then cooked down until it's a superthick and sweet syrup. Fake maple syrup, also known as pancake syrup, is basically maple-flavored sugar. Always try to use the highest-level and freshest ingredients in your cocktails for the best flavor possible.

dr. funk

A cocktail made popular by Don the Beachcomber and Trader Vic, the Dr. Funk is based on a drink invented by the German-born Dr. Bernard Funk of Samoa. It is most likely that he created this drink as some kind of medicinal tonic. It can be said that this drink was tiki before tiki was tiki. Originally, it was a mixture of absinthe, lime juice and seltzer. Rum didn't come into the picture until Don and Vic got their hands on this recipe, making it officially tiki. It's boozy, sweet, delightfully tart and herbal from the absinthe, but still simple enough to make, as far as tiki drinks go. This is an adapted recipe from Don the Beachcomber from the 1940s.

Makes 1 serving

2 oz (60 ml) Bermuda rum or dark Jamaican rum
¾ oz (22 ml) fresh lime juice
¾ oz (22 ml) Grenadine (page 183)
2 dashes of absinthe
Lime wheel, for garnish
Luxardo cherry, for garnish

In a cocktail shaker, combine the rum, lime juice, grenadine and absinthe, dry shake and pour into a Collins glass filled with ice. Swizzle and top with more crushed ice. Garnish with the lime wheel and cherry.

bartender's tip: If you want this drink to be sweet and rich, use a Bermuda rum, such as Gosling's. If you're leaning toward wanting this drink to be funkier, I would suggest going the Jamaican route.

bin 'n' gitters

This simple gimlet variation served on crushed ice is sour, slightly bitter and refreshing. This drink is adapted from The South American Gentlemen's Companion, *by Charles H. Baker, circa 1951. The recipe calls for four dashes of Angostura bitters, but I suggest going heavy handed to give the cocktail a bit more of a kick. Somewhere between four and ten dashes should do the trick, based on how bitter and aromatic you'd like to make your drink.*

Makes 1 serving

2 oz (60 ml) gin
1 oz (30 ml) fresh lime juice
½ oz (15 ml) Simple Syrup (page 179)
4 dashes of Angostura bitters
Mint sprig, for garnish

In a cocktail shaker, combine the gin, lime juice and simple syrup, dry shake and transfer to a double rocks glass over crushed ice. Swizzle and top with the bitters. Garnish with the mint spring.

captain's grog

This drink comes from the Hukilau Room of the Captain's Inn in Long Beach, California, circa the 1960s. It's a very rich ten-ingredient tiki drink that is well worth the effort. Despite a plethora of flavors competing to be up front in this cocktail, they integrate very nicely. I lean toward something like Appleton 12 Year for the Jamaican rum in this cocktail. It has a distinct funky note, but also brings a lot of oak and molasses flavor without being too assertive. You might want to make sure that you don't have anywhere to be after having one of these.

Makes 1 serving

½ oz (15 ml) Jamaican rum
½ oz (15 ml) aged rum
½ oz (15 ml) white rum
¼ oz (7 ml) falernum
¼ oz (7 ml) curaçao
¼ oz (7 ml) pure maple syrup
¾ oz (22 ml) fresh grapefruit juice
½ oz (15 ml) fresh lime juice
¼ oz (7 ml) Orgeat (page 184)
¼ oz (7 ml) Vanilla Syrup (page 181)
Freshly grated cinnamon, for garnish
Lime wheel, for garnish
3 Luxardo cherries, for garnish
Orchid, for garnish

In a cocktail shaker, combine the rums, falernum, curaçao, maple syrup, grapefruit juice, lime juice, orgeat and vanilla syrup, dry shake and pour into a Collins glass over crushed ice. Swizzle and top with crushed ice again. Garnish with freshly grated cinnamon and the lime wheel, cherries and orchid.

duke's pearl

Created by Duke Kahanamoku of Duke's Supper Club in Waikiki, 1963. Every fifth drink was served with an actual pearl. Duke was Hawaii's most famous surfer and a gold medalist in swimming at the 1912 and 1920 Olympics. I love the use of honey with passion fruit because it cuts the tartness quite a bit, to really smooth out the flavors in this potent libation. Impress your guests at your next tropical party and make these with a pearl garnish just the way Duke did at his supper club.

Makes 1 serving

2 oz (60 ml) aged rum

½ oz (15 ml) fresh lime juice

½ oz (15 ml) Honey Syrup (page 179)

¼ oz (7 ml) Passion Fruit Syrup (page 184)

Lime wheel, for garnish

Orchid, for garnish

Pearl, for garnish (optional)

In a cocktail shaker, combine the rum, lime juice, honey syrup and passion fruit syrup, dry shake and pour into a Collins glass over ice. Top with crushed ice and garnish with the lime wheel and orchid. Place the pearl in the center of the flower, if desired.

kamehameha rum punch

Kamehameha—also known as Kamehameha the Great—was the head of a dynasty that ruled the Hawaiian Islands for more than a century. He conquered the Hawaiian Islands and formally established the Kingdom of Hawaii in 1810. Every year in Hawaii on June 11, Kamehameha Day, his statue is draped with lovely leis and flowers in his honor. This day and festival continue to pay tribute to Kamehameha and act to preserve and perpetuate the Hawaiian culture. The Kamehameha Rum Punch is aesthetically stunning because of the layering technique, which makes it a great representation for the beauty of Hawaii and this tradition. This drink recipe is adapted from Beachbum Berry's Sippin' Safari *and is credited to the Hotel King Kamehameha in Kona, Hawaii, with an origin of around 1960.*

Makes 1 serving

¾ oz (22 ml) blackberry puree
1 oz (30 ml) white rum
¾ oz (22 ml) fresh pineapple juice
¼ oz (7 ml) fresh lemon juice
½ oz (15 ml) Grenadine (page 183)
1 oz (30 ml) dark rum
Fresh pineapple wedge, for garnish
Blackberry, for garnish

Place the blackberry puree in the bottom of a Collins glass and top with crushed ice. In a cocktail shaker, combine the white rum, pineapple juice, lemon juice and grenadine and dry shake (without ice). Pour the drink over the crushed ice, swizzle and top with more crushed ice. Float the dark rum by pouring it on top. Garnish with the pineapple wedge and blackberry.

kon tiki
tropical itch

The Kon Tiki Tropical Itch is probably a variation on another cocktail called the Tropical Itch by Harry Yee at the Hilton Hawaiian Village resort in Waikiki back in 1957. This is certainly my favorite version of the Tropical Itch cocktail created at the Kon Tiki Restaurant in Cleveland, Ohio, in the 1960s. The original version by Harry Yee was garnished with an actual bamboo backscratcher. I will leave it up to you whether you want to actually scratch that itch. This cocktail is citrusy, wonderfully fruity from mango and has warm notes from the cinnamon and orgeat.

Makes 1 serving

1 oz (30 ml) white rum

1 oz (30 ml) gin

¾ oz (22 ml) fresh lime juice

½ oz (15 ml) Orgeat (page 184)

½ oz (15 ml) Cinnamon Syrup (page 181)

¼ oz (7 ml) mango puree

Freshly grated cinnamon, for garnish

Lime wheel, for garnish

Orchid, for garnish

In a cocktail shaker, combine the rum, gin, lime juice, orgeat, cinnamon syrup and mango puree, dry shake and pour into a Collins glass over crushed ice. Swizzle and top with more crushed ice. Garnish with freshly grated cinnamon, the lime wheel and the orchid.

schooner

This 1955 gem is the creation of the Four Winds in Seattle. The Four Winds was a boat turned pirate-themed restaurant that boasted a 24-foot (7.3-m)-tall pirate atop its pilothouse. The Schooner was its centerpiece tiki drink until the restaurant sank to the bottom of Lake Union in 1966. A restaurant that actually went under. Tiki historian Jeff "Beachbum" Berry unearthed the recipe and I adapted it from Beachbum Berry Remixed. The Schooner is a boozy and fruity rum concoction, but my favorite part about this drink is the use of port wine. Tawny port is full of delicious flavors, such as caramel, apricot, plum, raisin and walnut. Even used in small amounts, it adds enormous flavor and depth to cocktails.

Makes 1 serving

1 oz (30 ml) white rum

½ oz (15 ml) 151 rum

½ oz (15 ml) tawny port

1 oz (30 ml) fresh lime juice

½ oz (15 ml) Demerara Syrup (page 180)

½ oz (15 ml) papaya puree

Luxardo cherry, for garnish

Cocktail pick, for skewering cherry

Leafy mint sprig, for garnish

In a cocktail shaker, combine the rums, port, lime juice, demerara syrup and papaya puree, dry shake and pour into a Collins glass over crushed ice. Swizzle and top with more crushed ice. Garnish with a skewered cherry on a cocktail pick and a healthy bouquet of mint.

bartender's tip: Tawny port is a type of port that undergoes oxidative aging in a wooden barrel for between 8 and 50 years. Older versions of this port tend to be drier, whereas young versions tend to be more sweet and luscious. I recommend using something young, such as Taylor Fladgate 10 Year Old.

frozen & frosty

The drinks outlined in this chapter are some of my favorite frozen creations from the midcentury. Some are sweet and creamy and others are bright and citrusy, but they are all frosty and delicious. Frozen cocktails have a rich history, just like any other classic cocktail. Americans' love affair with frozen drinks took root sometime in the 1950s. This was for two main reasons. When the blender was first invented in the 1920s, it was considered a large, loud, dangerous device, but by the 1950s, after many redesigns, it had become a useful kitchen tool. World War II changed the priorities for a lot of American households. During the war, women had to take jobs outside the home, and when the war ended, many of those women wanted to keep their jobs. With consumerism on the rise, the blender became a common kitchen appliance in most American homes, to make household duties lighter.

During the same period of time, tiki culture started to flourish for similar reasons. The postwar economy meant Americans had more disposable income, and they were looking for an escape. Hawaii becoming a state in 1959 furthered the popularity of the tropical lifestyle as well. The science behind creating a successful frozen drink is based on two main things. The primary one is sweetness. Frozen drinks have a much higher water content because of dilution so more sweetener is required to translate flavors properly. The second one is ice. I always recommend using 6 to 8 ounces (170 to 227 g) of crushed ice when blending, to achieve the best texture.

Tools of the Trade

A high-powered blender, such as a Blendtec or Vitamix, is highly recommended for making the drinks in this chapter. These types of blenders produce the smoothest texture of drinks possible. Using crushed ice when making frozen drinks also helps achieve a nicely textured cocktail. As always, you will need your trusted jigger, too. The glassware needed is a tiki mug, a double rocks glass, a pineapple vessel, a snifter, a goblet and a large hurricane glass.

the pearl of
la paz

When creating this drink, I was originally inspired by the Lava Flow cocktail, a strawberry piña colada of sorts. This is a really great drink for someone who likes coconut but wants to try something different that's not too sweet or with rum. I named it after one of my favorite John Steinbeck novels, The Pearl. *Steinbeck's inspiration for the novel was from a Mexican folk tale from La Paz, Baja California Sur, Mexico.*

Makes 1 serving

¾ oz (22 ml) mezcal

¾ oz (22 ml) scotch

½ oz (15 ml) Campari

¾ oz (22 ml) fresh pineapple juice

½ oz (15 ml) fresh lime juice

⅜ oz (11 ml) Cinnamon Syrup (page 181)

⅜ oz (11 ml) Coconut Cream (page 185)

2 strawberries, for blending

Strawberry, for garnish

Pearl, for garnish

Freshly grated cinnamon, for garnish

In a blender pitcher, combine the mezcal, scotch, Campari, pineapple juice, lime juice, cinnamon syrup, coconut cream and strawberries with 6 to 8 ounces (170 to 227 g) of crushed ice and blend. To make the strawberry rose, with the bottom end of your strawberry pointing upwards, make a small slit to one side of the point, but do not cut all the way through. Use your knife to very gently curl the tip of the slice into a "petal" by pressing it back. Repeat on the other three sides until you have four "petals." Make another row right above the one you just made. To finish the rose, make a slit down the tip and press back gently to curl. Place the pearl in the middle of the rose. Pour the drink into a clear tiki mug and garnish with the strawberry rose, pearl and freshly grated cinnamon.

heart of gold

This is my variation on a Pieces of Eight cocktail, which was a drink from the Pieces of Eight restaurant located in Marina del Rey, California, circa 1962. The original drink calls for silver rum, demerara, lemon, lime and passion fruit. I made the drink a little bit warmer and spicier by using an aged cachaça, cinnamon and orgeat.

Makes 1 serving

2 oz (60 ml) Avuá Amburana Cachaça
⅜ oz (11 ml) fresh lime juice
⅜ oz (11 ml) fresh lemon juice
½ oz (15 ml) Orgeat (page 184)
¼ oz (7 ml) Passion Fruit Syrup (page 184)
¼ oz (7 ml) Cinnamon Syrup (page 181)
Orchid, for garnish
Freshly grated cinnamon, for garnish.

In a blender pitcher, combine the cachaça, lime juice, lemon juice, orgeat, passion fruit syrup and cinnamon syrup with 6 to 8 ounces (170 to 227 g) of crushed ice and blend. Pour into a double rocks glass and garnish with the orchid and freshly grated cinnamon.

piña colada

This is one of the world's and also one of my most favorite mixed drinks. The Caribe Hilton, a premier luxury hotel in San Juan, claims the piña colada was first served in its Beachcomber Bar in 1954 by bartender Ramón "Monchito" Marrero. Hotel management asked Marrero to create a signature cocktail that captured the flavors of Puerto Rico. He supposedly spent three months developing the recipe before perfecting this sweet, creamy concoction of rum, pineapple and coconut. After tasting one of them, Hollywood legend Joan Crawford reportedly said it was "better than slapping Bette Davis in the face." Now, that's a drink! The following is an adaptation and my favorite recipe for making the piña colada.

Makes 1 serving

1½ oz (44 ml) aged rum

1½ oz (44 ml) Coconut Cream (page 185)

1½ oz (44 ml) fresh pineapple juice

1 pineapple

Pineapple shell, for vessel (see tip)

Coconut flakes, for garnish

Orchid, for garnish

Cocktail umbrella, for garnish

In a blender pitcher, combine the rum, coconut cream and pineapple juice with 6 to 8 ounces (170 to 227 g) of crushed ice and blend. For extra flavor, add a few pineapple chunks. Pour into a hollowed-out pineapple shell. Garnish with coconut flakes, the orchid and a cocktail umbrella.

bartender's tip: To make the pineapple shell, you will need a corer. First, slice off the head of your pineapple. Place the hollow part of the pineapple corer over the core. Once in place, begin turning clockwise while pushing down, until you get to the bottom of the pineapple, but be sure to not cut all the way through. Pull the corer up and out to remove the insides of the pineapple, and reserve the pineapple flesh for another use or discard it. The core will remain in the middle of the pineapple and you can cut it away and discard it. Once you're left with a hollowed-out pineapple shell, I suggest putting it in the freezer for a few hours to let the vessel harden and become sturdier. You can make these ahead of time, depending on how many piña coladas you will be serving.

missionary's downfall

A drink that's refreshing, herbal and delicious? That's a drink I can most definitely get behind! Don the Beachcomber, the man who invented tiki drinks, created this one in 1940. In my eyes, this is one of Don's greatest masterpieces: a bright and fruity drink that marries fresh mint, pineapple, honey, peach brandy and rum for an icy, blended slice of heaven. As the name suggests—it will tempt anyone to take a sip.

Makes 1 serving

1½ oz (44 ml) white rum

½ oz (15 ml) peach brandy or liqueur

1 oz (30 ml) fresh pineapple juice

¾ oz (22 ml) fresh lime juice

¾ oz (22 ml) Honey Syrup (page 179)

10 fresh mint leaves, for blending

Fresh pineapple wedge, for garnish

Pineapple leaves, for garnish

Mint sprig, for garnish

In a blender pitcher, combine the rum, peach brandy, pineapple juice, lime juice, honey syrup and mint leaves with 6 to 8 ounces (170 to 227 g) of crushed ice and blend. Pour into a large hurricane glass and garnish with the pineapple wedge, pineapple leaves and mint sprig.

bartender's tip: Peach brandy can be hard to come by. If you can find it, Catoctin Creek puts one out, but if you can't track it down, Mathilde or Giffard peach liqueur will suffice.

hawaii kai treasure

The Hawaii Kai was the grande dame of New York Polynesian restaurants. The location at 1638 Broadway was over the historic Winter Garden Theatre and was originally Monte Proser's Beachcomber, a Don the Beachcomber rip-off, in the 1940s. The drink Hawaii Kai Treasure was created by the Hawaii Kai's chief mixologist in the 1960s. It's sweet, citrusy, slightly creamy and rich. The proper garnish for this drink is a gardenia with a pearl resting in its petals. The pearl must be the treasure insinuated in the name of this cocktail, but drinking it is a reward all its own!

Makes 1 serving

1½ oz (44 ml) white rum
¼ oz (7 ml) curaçao
½ oz (15 ml) fresh grapefruit juice
¼ oz (7 ml) fresh lime juice
½ oz (15 ml) heavy cream
½ oz (15 ml) Orgeat (page 184)
¼ oz (7 ml) Honey Syrup (page 179)
Pearl, for garnish
Orchid or gardenia, for garnish

In a blender pitcher, combine the rum, curaçao, grapefruit juice, lime juice, heavy cream, orgeat and honey syrup with 6 to 8 ounces (170 to 227 g) of crushed ice and blend. Pour into a goblet and then rest the pearl in the center of the orchid and place on the drink as a garnish.

bartender's tip: The Hawaii Kai Treasure was originally made with green curaçao. I've never seen a bottle of such a thing. It is best to instead use a good-quality curaçao, such as Pierre Ferrand; and, as for the white rum I love using, a Martinique or Haitian rum. You can even replace the rum with your whiskey of choice.

big bamboo

The Mai-Kai in Fort Lauderdale, Florida, had so many legendary tropical drinks. The Big Bamboo was one of the very best, believed to only have been available for members of the Okole Maluna Society. Okole maluna, meaning "bottom's up!" is a traditional Hawaiian toast. This society was more like a customer loyalty program where members received a special menu on which they charted their progress. The challenge was to try every cocktail on the menu, and as a reward, you got an exclusive treat called the Big Bamboo only available to program members. This recipe was revealed by Jeff "Beachbum" Berry in his 2007 book Sippin' Safari and created by Mariano Licudine, circa 1960.

Makes 1 serving

1 oz (30 ml) Virgin Island rum

½ oz (15 ml) Jamaican rum

½ oz (15 ml) fresh orange juice

½ oz (15 ml) fresh grapefruit juice

½ oz (15 ml) fresh lime juice

½ oz (15 ml) Passion Fruit Syrup (page 184)

2 dashes of Angostura bitters

Lime wheel, for garnish

Luxardo cherry, for garnish

Cocktail pick, for skewering garnishes

In a blender pitcher, combine the rums, orange juice, grapefruit juice, lime juice, passion fruit syrup and bitters with 6 to 8 ounces (170 to 227 g) of crushed ice and blend. Pour into a mug and garnish with the skewered lime wheel and cherry.

cocoanut grove

This cocktail is from a legendary Hollywood haunt, the Cocoanut Grove in the Ambassador Hotel in Los Angeles, California, circa the 1940s. A supper club where the rich and famous dined and danced, in its day it was filled with artificial palm trees, papier-mâché coconuts and stuffed monkeys that came from the set of the Rudolph Valentino movie The Sheik. The Academy Awards took place there in 1930, as did the first Golden Globe Awards. Nightly entertainment consisted of such talent as Fanny Brice, W. C. Fields, Nat King Cole and Judy Garland. The Cocoanut Grove cocktail is somewhat of a Creamsicle-meets–piña colada. While you sip it, pretend you're underneath those palm fronds, dancing with the best of them.

Makes 1 serving

1½ oz (44 ml) white rum
½ oz (15 ml) Coconut Cream (page 185)
½ oz (15 ml) curaçao
½ oz (15 ml) fresh lime juice
Orange slice, for garnish
Luxardo cherry, for garnish
Orchid, for garnish

In a blender pitcher, combine the rum, coconut cream, curaçao and lime juice with 6 to 8 ounces (170 to 227 g) of crushed ice and blend. Pour into a goblet and garnish with the orange slice, cherry and orchid.

never say die

Another rich, robust and refreshing beverage from Don the Beachcomber, circa the 1960s, discovered in Jeff "Beachbum" Berry's 2013 Grog Log *and 2009* Remixed. *This is an ambitious libation with nine ingredients, yet the drink is somewhat mild in alcohol while sweet, citrusy and bright in flavor. The drink's moniker, Never Say Die, has been around since the 1800s. An early-published example of the saying is from "A Man of War's Man" in* Blackwood's Magazine *in 1825. The wartime expression is "Cheer up then, and never say die, for the devil a morsel of good it will do." This demonstrates the yearning for escapism during economic depression and war in the midcentury.*

Makes 1 serving

½ oz (15 ml) Jamaican rum
½ oz (15 ml) Barbados rum
½ oz (15 ml) white rum
¾ oz (22 ml) fresh pineapple juice
¼ oz (7 ml) fresh grapefruit juice
¼ oz (7 ml) fresh orange juice
¼ oz (7 ml) fresh lime juice
¾ oz (22 ml) Honey Syrup (page 179)
Dash of Angostura bitters
Fresh pineapple wedge, for garnish
Pineapple leaves, for garnish
Luxardo cherry, for garnish

In a blender pitcher, combine the rums, pineapple juice, grapefruit juice, orange juice, lime juice, honey syrup and bitters with 6 to 8 ounces (170 to 227 g) of crushed ice and blend. Pour into a snifter glass and garnish with the pineapple wedge, pineapple leaves and cherry.

piña paradise

This drink was invented in Miami in 1955 at Sam Denning's Club Luau, and there advertised as "number one on the sip parade." I discovered this in Jeff "Beachbum" Berry's 2007 Sippin' Safari. By its name, you might relate this one to a piña colada, but they are in no way the same. This is a deeply citrusy and refreshing drink and a great opportunity to introduce people to rhum agricole without overwhelming them. Make yourself one and join the parade!

Makes 1 serving

¾ oz (22 ml) Martinique rhum

¾ oz (22 ml) Puerto Rican rum

½ oz (15 ml) fresh pineapple juice

¼ oz (7 ml) fresh orange juice

¼ oz (7 ml) fresh grapefruit juice

¼ oz (7 ml) fresh lime juice

½ oz (15 ml) Demerara Syrup (page 180)

¼ oz (7 ml) Orgeat (page 184)

Dash of Angostura bitters

Fresh pineapple wedge, for garnish

Pineapple leaves, for garnish

Orange wheel, for garnish

Luxardo cherry, for garnish

In a blender pitcher, combine the rums, pineapple juice, orange juice, grapefruit juice, lime juice, demerara syrup, orgeat and bitters with 6 to 8 ounces (170 to 227 g) of crushed ice and blend. Pour into a Collins or a clear pineapple mug and garnish with the pineapple wedge, pineapple leaves, orange wheel and cherry.

polynesian paralysis

This is a midcentury recipe from Hawaii. It originally called for okolehao, which is a Hawaiian spirit that is not easy to acquire. I suggest using bourbon or rye as a substitution. If you prefer drinks to be sweeter, I recommend using bourbon here, and rye if you want to add a bit of spice. Overall, the juice and citrus combination make this drink bright and fruity, while the orgeat and demerara syrup add depth and richness.

Makes 1 serving

1½ oz (44 ml) bourbon or rye whiskey
1½ oz (44 ml) fresh pineapple juice
½ oz (15 ml) fresh lemon juice
½ oz (15 ml) fresh orange juice
½ oz (15 ml) Orgeat (page 184)
¼ oz (7 ml) Demerara Syrup (page 180)
Orchid, for garnish

In a blender pitcher, combine the whiskey, pineapple juice, lemon juice, orange juice, orgeat and demerara syrup with 6 to 8 ounces (170 to 227 g) of crushed ice and blend. Pour into a goblet and garnish with the orchid.

bartender's tip: If you're feeling adventurous, a great riff on this drink is one by Martin Cate from Smuggler's Cove in San Francisco, California, called the Norwegian Paralysis. It calls for aquavit instead of bourbon or rye, for a beautiful balance of sweet and savory.

port light

I love seeing bourbon as an ingredient in tiki cocktails because it just wasn't used in this style of drink as much as rum was. This is also a pretty simple drink as far as tiki cocktails go. The combination of both passion fruit and grenadine make this cocktail a fun, fruity approach to a whiskey sour, and hopefully its flavor will let you set sail to Tahiti. The Port Light was the brainchild of Sandro Conti of the Kahiki Supper Club in Columbus, Ohio, circa 1961.

Makes 1 serving

1 ½ oz (44 ml) bourbon
¾ oz (22 ml) fresh lemon juice
½ oz (15 ml) Passion Fruit Syrup (page 184)
¼ oz (7 ml) Grenadine (page 183)
Cocktail pick, for skewering garnishes
Luxardo cherry, for garnish
Lemon wheel, for garnish

In a blender pitcher, combine the bourbon, lemon juice, passion fruit syrup and grenadine with 6 to 8 ounces (170 to 227 g) of crushed ice and blend. Pour into a goblet and garnish with the skewered cherry and lemon wheel.

bartender's note: Lee Henry started the Kahiki with Bill Sapp after their original tiki bar, the Grass Shack, burned down in 1959. They conceived building one of the largest Polynesian restaurants in the United States and had Columbus architect Coburn Morgan build it in 1960. It held over 500 guests and had waterfalls, fish tanks, live birds, an iconic monkey fountain known as George and a giant stone Moai fireplace.

frothy &
foamy

As America's youth sipped on milkshakes at the soda fountain, their parents downed dessert and egg cocktails at the bar. Using eggs in cocktails can be traced back to the Golden Age of Cocktails in the late 19th century, but a lot of recipes didn't deviate far from eggnog. Eggs in cocktails really started to take shape in the twentieth century, and drinks such as the whiskey sour, although not created in the midcentury, were a popular drink at that time. Drinks that contain egg white only are fizzes and traditional sours. If they contain a whole egg or just the yolk, they're called a flip. So, why use eggs in cocktails? First, they provide a silky and foamy body that feels rich on the tongue. Egg white drinks provide a frothy cap to a drink, like the foam on a latte. Much as a barista may decorate latte foam with shapes and patterns, a bartender can use drops of bitters to decorate an egg white cocktail. Second, using yolks or whole eggs in drinks provides a more "noggy" flavor that is rich and creamy.

Mixing egg cocktails requires a little extra work because you need to emulsify the ingredients. Traditionally, you accomplish this by building the drink, dry shaking without ice and then shaking it again with ice to chill and dilute the drink.

Tools of the Trade

To make the drinks in this chapter, or other drinks that contain eggs or dairy, it is best to use a Boston shaker. This type of shaker, which has two sides, allows you to separate your dairy or eggs from the rest of your cocktail until you are ready to mix, to avoid curdling of any kind. You will need a jigger to measure your ingredients— and your muscles, because you're going to be doing a lot of shaking. The glassware needed is a coupe glass and a Collins or highball glass.

sunny-side up fizz

When I was developing this drink, I was very inspired by midcentury soda fountains of the 1950s. I frequented one that's been around since the '50s for breakfast or lunch simply to be transported back in time. Not only was I inspired by the location, but also by the types of food and drinks one enjoys at luncheonettes, such as breakfast, coffee, milkshakes and egg creams. The Sunny-Side Up Fizz is a fizz-meets-flip because of the use of a whole egg instead of just the white of the egg. A pinch of cayenne adds some spice and makes this the perfect sweet and savory breakfast or brunch drink.

Makes 1 serving

1½ oz (44 ml) reposado tequila
¾ oz (22 ml) coffee liqueur
½ oz (15 ml) Cinnamon Syrup (page 181)
1 large egg
Club soda
Pinch of cayenne pepper, for garnish

In the small side of your Boston cocktail shaker, combine the tequila, coffee liqueur and cinnamon syrup. Place your egg in the larger side of your tin and dry shake (without ice) for 10 seconds to emulsify the egg. Fill your shaker with ice and vigorously shake again. Strain into a highball glass and top with club soda. Garnish with a pinch of cayenne.

apple
blow fizz

There's nothing more refreshing than a bright snap of citrus and some bubbles. The Apple Blow Fizz has both of these qualities with the addition of warmth like your favorite cozy sweater. That is because instead of using a base of gin, this fizz is built on apple brandy. Its depth of flavor and warming qualities, especially if you use the 100-proof kind, makes it the perfect cool-weather fizz option. From The Fine Art of Mixing Drinks, *by David Embury, circa 1948.*

Makes 1 serving

2 oz (60 ml) applejack
¾ oz (22 ml) fresh lemon juice
¾ oz (22 ml) Simple Syrup (page 179)
1 large egg white
Club soda

In the small side of your Boston cocktail shaker, combine the applejack, lemon juice and simple syrup. Place your egg white in the larger side of your tin and dry shake (without ice) for about 10 seconds to emulsify the egg white. Fill your shaker with ice and vigorously shake again. Strain into a highball glass and top with club soda. The soda should produce a very thick and foamy head.

bumble bee

This drink is a Honeysuckle cocktail (honey daiquiri) with the addition of an egg white. The Bumble Bee is frothy, rich and bright, which makes it perfect for the person with a sweet tooth. A simple drink from Charles H. Baker's The South American Gentleman's Companion, circa 1951, that's full of flavor and worthy of making it into your drink rotation.

Makes 1 serving

2 oz (60 ml) aged rum

¾ oz (22 ml) fresh lime juice

¾ oz (22 ml) Honey Syrup (page 179)

1 large egg white

Dash of Angostura bitters, for garnish

In the small side of your Boston cocktail shaker, combine the rum, lime juice and honey syrup. Place your egg white in the larger side of your tin and dry shake (without ice) for about 10 seconds to emulsify the egg white. Fill your shaker with ice and vigorously shake again. Strain into a coupe glass and then drop your dash of bitters on top.

bartender's tips: I usually make this with Plantation Original Dark Rum, but if you want to get funky, try using a more forward Jamaican rum, such as Appleton or Smith & Cross. You can also use multiple dashes of Angostura bitters to create a design on top of the egg white foam.

chanticleer

This drink from Trader Vic's Bartender's Guide, circa 1947, is almost a spitting image of a classic Clover Club cocktail. The only difference is the absence of dry vermouth. To be honest, I love this particular version because there's no vermouth in it. The Chanticleer is beautifully simple but smooth, fruity and delicious. It is a great choice to make in the spring or warmer months.

Makes 1 serving

2 oz (60 ml) gin
¾ oz (22 ml) fresh lemon juice
¾ oz (22 ml) Simple Syrup (page 179)
5 raspberries, plus more for garnish
1 large egg white
Cocktail pick, for skewering raspberries

In the small side of your Boston cocktail shaker, combine the gin, lemon juice, simple syrup and 5 raspberries and muddle lightly (bruise, don't abuse). Place your egg white in the larger side of your tin and dry shake (without ice) for about 10 seconds to emulsify the egg white. Fill your shaker with ice and vigorously shake again. Strain into a coupe glass and garnish with a few whole raspberries on a cocktail pick.

georgetown demerara flip

Adapted from The South American Gentleman's Companion, *by Charles H. Baker, published in 1951, this recipe originally came from Baker's travels in British Guyana. He described it as "a mild quick and easy picker-upper." The original version of this drink contained canned evaporated milk because fresh milk or cream was rare in Georgetown. I re-created the recipe here to contain heavy cream for the sake of flavor and added sweetener, as the original version didn't have any.*

Makes 1 serving

1 oz (30 ml) demerara rum
½ oz (15 ml) 151 demerara rum
½ oz (15 ml) Pedro Ximénez sherry
½ oz (15 ml) heavy cream
¼ oz (7 ml) fresh lime juice
¼ oz (7 ml) Demerara Syrup (page 180)
1 large egg
Freshly grated nutmeg, for garnish

In the small side of your Boston cocktail shaker, combine the rums, sherry, heavy cream, lime juice and demerara syrup. Place your egg in the larger side of your tin and dry shake (without ice) for about 10 seconds to emulsify the egg. Fill your shaker with ice and vigorously shake again. Strain into a coupe glass and garnish with freshly grated nutmeg.

imperial hotel fizz

This drink was originally created using rum from Saint Croix, but I tend to like to make this one with a high-proof pot-still Jamaican rum, such as Smith & Cross. The funkiness of the Jamaican rum mixed with the spiciness of a rye whiskey makes a simple cocktail like this have a really deep, interesting and complex flavor. It is adapted from the 1940 edition of The Official Mixer's Manual, *by Patrick Gavin Duffy.*

Makes 1 serving

1 oz (30 ml) rye whiskey
1 oz (30 ml) Jamaican rum
¾ oz (22 ml) fresh lemon juice
¾ oz (22 ml) Simple Syrup (page 179)
1 large egg white
Sparkling water

In the small side of your Boston cocktail shaker, combine the whiskey, rum, lemon juice and simple syrup. Place your egg white in the larger side of your tin and dry shake (without ice) for about 10 seconds to emulsify the egg white. Fill your shaker with ice and vigorously shake again. Strain into a highball glass and top with sparkling water.

itchiban

A flip is a cocktail that has the yolk of one egg or sometimes just the whole damn egg! Here is a boozy flip reminiscent of a Brandy Alexander from Trader Vic's Bartender's Guide, circa 1947. Although not as creamy for the lack of heavy cream in this recipe, the whole egg provides a creamy texture and silky mouthfeel.

Makes 1 serving

2 oz (60 ml) cognac
½ oz (15 ml) crème de cacao
½ oz (15 ml) Bénédictine
1 large egg
Freshly grated nutmeg, for garnish

In the small side of your Boston cocktail shaker, combine the cognac, crème de cacao and Bénédictine. Place your egg in the larger side of your tin and dry shake (without ice) for about 10 seconds to emulsify the egg. Fill your shaker with ice and vigorously shake again. Strain into a coupe glass and garnish with freshly grated nutmeg.

bartender's tip: The original recipe calls for white crème de cacao but I'm rather a fan of the dark stuff. Tempus Fugit Dark Crème de Cacao is always my go-to for this recipe.

snow white

This is an egg white version of a pineapple daiquiri, which is perhaps one of the most delightful drinks in existence. Shaken cocktails with fresh pineapple juice always produce a decadent head on top of drinks because of all the enzymes present in pineapple juice. Add an egg white and you have an explosion of foamy goodness. It is adapted from The Fine Art of Mixing Drinks, *by David Embury, circa 1948.*

Makes 1 serving

1½ oz (44 ml) white rum
1 oz (30 ml) fresh pineapple juice
½ oz (15 ml) fresh lime juice
½ oz (15 ml) Simple Syrup (page 179)
1 large egg white
Fresh pineapple slice, for garnish

In the small side of your Boston cocktail shaker, combine the rum, pineapple juice, lime juice and simple syrup. Place your egg white in the larger side of your tin and dry shake (without ice) for about 10 seconds to emulsify the egg white. Fill your shaker with ice and vigorously shake again. Strain into a coupe glass and garnish with the pineapple slice.

bartender's tip: Using white rum, such as Plantation 3 Star, is preferable here, and if you want to try something more adventurous and funky, use a Haitian- or Martinique-style rum.

trade wind cocktail

The drink was invented at the Trade Winds Restaurant of Watermill, Long Island, New York, in 1959. This is a Gin Sour variation that is sweet, citrusy and bright. I feel that a lot of egg white drinks from this time period can be a bit heavy and dessertlike. This cocktail stands out because of its lighter profile and it is a great simple egg white drink to enjoy in the warmer months.

Makes 1 serving

1½ oz (44 ml) gin
½ oz (15 ml) curaçao
¾ oz (22 ml) fresh lemon juice
¼ oz (7 ml) Demerara Syrup (page 180)
1 large egg white

In the small side of your Boston cocktail shaker, combine the gin, curaçao, lemon juice and demerara syrup. Place your egg white in the larger side of your tin and dry shake (without ice) for about 10 seconds to emulsify the egg white. Fill your shaker with ice and vigorously shake again. Strain into a coupe glass.

punches & party drinks

I hear clinking glasses, soft laughter and easygoing melodies filling the air—did someone say "party"? The history of punch dates back to the 1600s, but the mid-twentieth century was known for its at-home dinner and cocktail parties. Having a great large-format recipe up your sleeve for entertaining is a must. The punch bowl is great for all manners of occasions, whether for holidays, formal or informal get-togethers and all other at-home occasions throughout the year.

There are a few things to consider when making punch. First of all, use only the best-quality spirits. You should always be looking to get the best flavor when you're making drinks. Second, always use fresh juice, fresh fruit and homemade syrups. Always! The last thing is, always use clean, clear large-format ice to keep your punch chilled. A great tip for making excellent punch is to blend your fruit, juices, liquors or wines in advance and let them chill in the refrigerator for at least an hour. Cold liquids are less likely to melt ice and then they will not quickly dilute the punch. When ready to serve, pour the chilled mixture over a block of ice and then add your carbonated elements, such as Champagne or club soda.

Tools of the Trade

No punch or party would be complete without a flowing bowl or large serving vessel of sorts. If serving from a bowl, make sure you have a ladle and punch cups. Over the years, I have found many full punch sets at my local Salvation Army or Goodwill. Thrift stores are a great place to find affordable vintage glassware. Always use a measuring cup or jigger to measure out all your ingredients. Using large-format ice is always best for a punch, to keep it as cold as possible while it sits out.

midcentury pink tea party

Millennial pink, otherwise known as blush or delicate pink, is a trend that showed up a few years ago and simply will not go away. Could it be that the midcentury furniture and design craze is partially to blame for this? Pink was, in fact, one of the most popular colors of the 1950s and '60s, covering clothes, furniture, carpeting and even kitchen appliances. I took inspiration from my favorite color and the connection of its popularity now (and then) for this punch, which also nods to party punches of the midcentury. This wine-based punch is light, fruity, refreshing and delightfully citrusy making it perfect for warmer weather or serving at a brunch party.

Makes 4 to 6 servings

7 oz (207 ml) rosé wine

3 oz (89 ml) Aperol

3 oz (89 ml) pamplemousse liqueur

3 oz (89 ml) Hibiscus Syrup (page 182)

1 oz (30 ml) fresh grapefruit juice

1 oz (30 ml) fresh lemon juice

Sparkling wine

Teapot, for serving

Teacups, for serving

Pansies, for garnish

In a teapot, combine the rosé wine, Aperol, pamplemousse liqueur, hibiscus syrup, grapefruit juice and lemon juice. Add crushed ice and mix with a bar spoon or swizzle stick. Top with sparkling wine and place the lid on the teapot. In each of your teacups, place a pansy and pour the punch on top.

bartender's tip: If you'd like to make this punch larger to serve more people, simply double the recipe and serve it in a bowl instead of a teapot.

strawberry champagne bowler

This is a go-to for summer parties because it's really easy to throw together and is an absolute crowd-pleaser. Who doesn't love strawberries and Champagne? No one, I hope, because it is possibly one of the best flavor combinations ever. I would suggest using a dry white wine, such as a chardonnay or a sauvignon blanc. I adapted this very simple yet delicious Champagne punch from the circa-1941 Here's How, *by W. C. Whitfield.*

Makes 12 servings

8 oz (237 g) strawberries, hulled and sliced

2 tbsp (25 g) sugar

2 oz (60 ml) cognac

2 (1-L) bottles white wine

2 (1-L) bottles Champagne

In a punch bowl, crush the strawberries into the sugar by using a muddler and then pour in the cognac and 8 ounces (237 ml) of the white wine; let this stand for about 1 hour. When ready to serve, add a large block of ice and then pour in the remainder of the white wine and both bottles of Champagne. Stir and serve.

bartender's tip: Other fresh fruit that is in season may be used in place of the strawberries.

society punch

Very potent but delightful, this recipe combines some of my favorite things to use in punch: cognac, rum, tea and Champagne. Using tea in punch has so many benefits, including adding depth of flavor and a caffeinated element. This punch is strong, flavorful, fruity and effervescent. This is a recipe adapted from The South American Gentleman's Companion, *by Charles H. Baker, circa 1951.*

Makes 12 servings

1 pineapple, peeled, cored and sliced

Juice of 6 lemons

4 oz (113 g) sugar

8 oz (237 ml) cognac

2 oz (60 ml) Jamaican rum

1 pint (475 ml) brewed green tea

2 oz (60 ml) peach liqueur

1 (1-L) bottle Champagne

2 qt (2 L) club soda

Lemon wheels, for garnish

In a punch bowl, combine the sliced pineapple with the lemon juice, sugar and cognac. Let stand for up to 1 hour or longer. When ready to serve, add the rum, green tea, peach liqueur, Champagne and club soda. Garnish with lemon wheels. Stir and serve.

trader vic's 1946 scorpion bowl

The Scorpion, like many tiki drinks, has gone through countless iterations over the years. This one is Trader Vic's 1946 version that I made during my time behind the bar at PKNY in New York City. It is thought that this drink was modeled after a punch that Vic tried on a trip to Hawaii with okolehao, an indigenous spirit distilled from the Polynesian ti plant. The richness of orgeat plays an important role in balancing the rum and citrus in this drink. This is a boozy, sweet and fun drink that will impress all of your friends when you set the bowl ablaze.

Serves 6 to 8

10 oz (296 ml) aged rum

2 oz (60 ml) cognac

4 oz (120 ml) fresh lemon juice

3 oz (89 ml) fresh orange juice

3 oz (89 ml) Orgeat (page 184)

151 rum, for bowl

Freshly grated cinnamon, for garnish

Orchids, for garnish

In a blender pitcher, combine the aged rum, cognac, lemon juice, orange juice and orgeat. Add 6 ounces (170 g) of crushed ice and blend. This is for dilution and nothing else; we are not trying to make this frozen. Fill the top of a volcano bowl with 151 rum and set ablaze with a lighter, then grate a pinch of cinnamon into the bowl. Pour the drink into the scorpion bowl along with a few pieces of ice. Garnish with orchids.

syrups

simple syrup

Makes 1 cup (240 ml) syrup

½ cup (100 g) sugar
½ cup (120 ml) hot (not boiling) water

In a heatproof container, combine the sugar and hot water and stir until all the sugar has dissolved. You do not need to bring this to a boil because that causes liquid to evaporate and may affect the taste of your cocktails. Cover and refrigerate for up to 2 weeks.

honey syrup

Makes 1⅓ cups (320 ml) syrup

1 cup (240 ml) honey
⅓ cup (80 ml) hot (not boiling) water

In a heatproof container, combine the honey and hot water and stir until the honey is completely incorporated. Cover and refrigerate for up to 2 weeks.

ginger syrup

Makes 1 cup (240 ml) syrup

½ cup (120 ml) fresh ginger juice (see tip)
½ cup (100 g) sugar

In a small saucepan, combine the ginger juice and sugar and simmer over low heat, stirring, just until all the sugar has dissolved. Remove from the heat, let cool completely, cover and refrigerate for up to 1 week.

bartender's tip: Use a slow juicer to extract the ginger juice. You will need about 1 large 6-inch (15-cm)-long piece of fresh ginger to extract ½ cup (120 ml) of juice.

demerara syrup

Makes 1½ cups (360 ml) syrup

1 cup (200 g) demerara sugar
½ cup (120 ml) water

In a small saucepan, combine the demerara sugar and water and simmer over low heat, stirring, just until all the sugar has dissolved. Remove from the heat, let cool completely, cover and refrigerate for up to 2 weeks.

cinnamon syrup

Makes 1½ cups (360 ml) syrup

1 cup (200 g) demerara sugar
½ cup (120 ml) water
4 cinnamon sticks

In a small saucepan, combine the demerara sugar, water and cinnamon sticks and simmer over low heat, stirring, just until all the sugar has dissolved. Remove from the heat. Let the cinnamon sticks steep while the syrup cools and then strain out and discard the cinnamon sticks. Cover and refrigerate for up to 2 weeks.

vanilla syrup

Makes 1 cup (240 ml) syrup

½ cup (100 g) sugar
½ cup (120 ml) hot water
2 vanilla beans, cut in half

In a small saucepan, combine the sugar, water and vanilla beans and simmer over low heat, stirring, just until all the sugar has dissolved. Remove from the heat. Let the vanilla beans steep while the syrup cools and then strain out and discard the vanilla beans. Cover and refrigerate for up to 2 weeks.

pineapple syrup

Makes 1½ cups (360 ml) syrup

1 cup (200 g) demerara sugar
½ cup (120 ml) water
1 cup (165 g) fresh pineapple chunks

In a small saucepan, combine the demerara sugar, water and pineapple. Simmer over low heat, stirring, just until all the sugar has dissolved. Remove from the heat and let cool completely. Strain out and discard the pineapple chunks, cover and refrigerate for up to 2 weeks.

hibiscus syrup

Makes 1 cup (240 ml) syrup

½ cup (100 g) sugar
½ cup (120 ml) water
½ cup (100 g) dried hibiscus flowers

In a small saucepan, combine the sugar, water and hibiscus flowers. Simmer over low heat, stirring, just until all the sugar has dissolved. Remove from the heat and let cool completely. Strain out and discard the hibiscus flowers, cover and refrigerate for up to 2 weeks.

bartender's tip: Most Latin markets and health food stores carry dried hibiscus flowers. In Latin markets, they are called *flor de Jamaica*.

hibiscus—habanero syrup

Makes 1 cup (240 ml) syrup

½ cup (100 g) sugar
½ cup (120 ml) water
½ cup (100 g) dried hibiscus flowers
3 fresh habanero peppers, cut in half lengthwise

In a small saucepan, combine the sugar, water, hibiscus flowers and habanero peppers and simmer over low heat, stirring, until all the sugar has dissolved. Remove from the heat and let steep for 10 more minutes. Let cool completely, then strain out and discard the hibiscus flowers and habanero peppers. Transfer to a sealed jar or bottle and refrigerate for up to 2 weeks.

grenadine

Makes 10 oz (296 ml) syrup

9 oz (270 ml) Simple Syrup (page 179)
1 oz (30 ml) pomegranate molasses
1 bar spoon (1 tsp) orange flower water

In a container, combine the simple syrup, pomegranate molasses and orange flower water and stir until incorporated. Cover and refrigerate for up to 2 weeks.

passion fruit syrup

Makes 1 cup (240 ml) syrup

½ cup (120 ml) passion fruit puree
½ cup (120 ml) Demerara Syrup (page 180)

In a container, combine the passion fruit puree with the demerara syrup and stir until incorporated.

bartender's tip: I'm a big fan of The Perfect Purée of Napa Valley products. If you can't make your puree fresh, especially because passion fruit is hard to come by, I strongly suggest using this brand for passion fruit, mango, papaya and blackberry purees.

orgeat

Makes 1 cup (240 ml) syrup

1 cup (200 g) almonds
2 cups (480 ml) water, divided
2 cups (440 g) demerara sugar
¼ tsp almond extract
1 bar spoon (1 tsp) orange flower water

In a bowl, soak the almonds in 1 cup (240 ml) of the water overnight or for 6 to 8 hours. This makes the nuts softer for optimal juicing. Strain out the water and rinse the almonds. Add the remaining cup (240 ml) of fresh water to the bowl. Using a measuring cup, spoon the almond mixture into a slow juicer as the juicer runs. Keep adding until you've put in all of the almond mixture. Let all the almond milk flow out of the juicer into a bowl and then transfer to a small saucepan and add the demerara sugar to the almond milk. Simmer over low heat until all the sugar has dissolved. Remove from the heat and add the almond extract and orange flower water. Let completely cool, then cover and refrigerate for up to 2 weeks.

bartender's tip: If you don't have a slow juicer, you can make the almond mixture in a high-speed blender. This will require an extra step of straining the milk through a cheesecloth before adding the demerara sugar and heating on the stove.

coconut cream

Makes 5½ cups (1.3 L) coconut cream

2 (15-oz [425-g]) cans Coco López cream of coconut
1 (14-oz [414-ml]) can coconut milk

In a small saucepan, combine the cream of coconut and the coconut milk and simmer over low heat until incorporated. Remove from the heat, let completely cool, cover and refrigerate for up to 2 weeks. You will need to let this come to room temperature before using.

acknowledgments

I would like to gratefully acknowledge my mother, father, sister, brother and my whole family. My two cats, Erik and Dolly Parton and my Chinese Crested dog, David Bowie, for without them life would be all too lonely. I would like to thank all of my readers and followers of my blog for all their continued support over these last few years. Without each and every one of you this book and my work would not be possible. I would like to thank Richard Boccato and the entire Dutch Kills family and every person that I have ever worked with there. In my eyes, Dutch Kills is the best bar in the world and I have been blessed to call that bar my home for eight years. Sasha Petraske, because without him, none of us would be here. Jeff Berry for dedicating his life to the history of tiki. The ghosts of PKNY, Lani Kai and the OG NYC tikiphiles. I would also like to thank Julie Reiner and Ryan Mcgrale (who is no longer with us) for taking a chance on a silly nightclub bartender and allowing me to pursue my passion of making cocktails. Further gratitude to the Page Street Publishing family, Elsie Larson, Emma Chapman and the A Beautiful Mess family, Katy Carrier of Palm Springs Style, Jess Weeks, Kent Baker, Jen Scott and my whole Archer family, Wilson Oliver for bringing me coffee and being my photo assistant while shooting this book, the Mathews family, Barcade family, Jay Zimmerman and the Ba'sik family, Brandon Bramhall and the Attaboy family, my best friend Samantha Withers and her husband, Jonathan Withers, Janna Narke, Dana Skinner, Mariah Kunkel, Alain Joseph and Drew Horne.

about the author

natalie jacob is a professional bartender who has been working in the hospitality industry for seventeen years and bartending in cocktail bars in New York City for the last decade. She was born and raised in Hudson County, New Jersey, and currently lives in Jersey City, New Jersey. She runs her own beverage and creative consulting business along with writing for her own cocktail and lifestyle blog *Arsenic Lace*. When she's not developing pretty drinks, taking photos, writing or bartending, she's either decorating, listening to country music, at a flea market looking for vintage glassware or being a dog mom to her Chinese Crested David Bowie. Her drinks have been featured in *Imbibe Magazine*, *The Village Voice*, *Time Out New York*, *Business Insider*, *Edible Magazine*, *Beverage Media*, *Wine Enthusiast* and on Refinery29. She has also contributed recipes to A Beautiful Mess and Palm Springs Style.

index

index 191